IN MEMORIAM

SO·THE·HEART·BE·RIGHT

Joanna Defrates

1945-2000

TRANSPORT *in* ANCIENT EGYPT

For Peter Phillips

TRANSPORT
in ANCIENT
EGYPT

ROBERT PARTRIDGE

THE RUBICON PRESS

The Rubicon Press
57 Cornwall Gardens
London SW7 4BE

British Library Cataloguing in Publication Data

A catalogue record for this book is available from the British Library.

ISBN 0-948695-42-0 (hbk)
ISBN 0-948695-43-9 (pbk)

Designed and typeset by Screentype, London
Printed and bound in Great Britain by Biddles Limited of Guildford
and King's Lynn

Contents

List of Illustrations

Unless otherwise stated, all the line drawings are by the author and the photographs are from the author's collection.

Chronology and Principal Kings
mentioned in the text

The Pre-historic or Predynastic Period	**Before 3150 B.C**
Narmer	3150–3090 B.C.
The Archaic Period – Dynasties 1 and 2	**3150–2686 B.C.**
The Old Kingdom – Dynasties 3 to 6	**2686–2181 B.C.**
Dynasty 3. Djoser	2668–2649 B.C.
Dynasty 4. Khufu	2589–2566 B.C.
Khafra	2558–2532 B.C.
The First Intermediate Period Dynasties 7 to 10	**2040–1782 B.C.**
The Middle Kingdom – Dynasties 11 and 12	**2040–1782 B.C**
Dynasty 12. Senuseret I	1971–1928 B.C.
Senuseret II	1878–1841 B.C.
AmenemhatIII	1842–1797 B.C.
The Second Intermediate Period	**1782–1570 B.C**
The New Kingdom – Dynasties 18 and 20	**1570–1070 B.C.**
Dynasty 18. Amenhotep I	1551–1524 B.C.
Hatshepsut	1498–1483 B.C.
Thutmose III	1504–1450 B.C.
Amenhotep II	1453–1419 B.C.
Thutmose IV	1419–1386 B.C.
Amenhotep III	1386–1349 B.C.
Akhenaten	1350–1334 B.C
Tutankhamun	1334–1325 B.C.
Horemhe	1321–1293 B.C.
Dynasty 19. Seti I	1291–1278 B.C.
Rameses II	1279–1212 B.C.
Dynasty 20. Rameses III	1182–1151 B.C.
The Third Intermediate Period – Dynasties 21 to 26	**1070–525 B.C**
The Late Period – Dynaties 37 to 30	**525–332 B.C.**
The Graeco-Roman Period	**332 B.C–A.D. 323**
Alexander the Great	332–323 B.C.
Cleopatra VII	51–30 B.C.
Augustus	30 B.C.–A.D. 14

Adapted from *The Penguin Guide to Ancient Egypt*, by William J. Murnane

Preface

My interest in Ancient Egyptian boats was rekindled when I saw the reassembled boat of Khufu in its museum, adjacent to the Great Pyramid at Giza. This vessel is the most amazing and impressive of all the objects to have been discovered in Egypt. A huge undertaking, requiring the skills of many craftsmen to build and sail, it sums up the achievements of the civilisation. It was built early in Egypt's history, and for three thousand years, boats like it sailed up and down the river Nile and even further afield to neighbouring countries, carrying precious cargoes to and from Egypt.

The contents of Tutankhamun's tomb have not ceased to arouse interest since their discovery in 1922. I have always been fascinated by the chariots which were found dismantled in the small tomb, and was disappointed that there were few published illustrations of the reassembled ones.

On a visit to the Ashmolean Museum in Oxford, I was impressed by a fragment of a chariot wheel found in the tomb of Amenhotep III. Badly damaged and battered this object nevertheless is a masterpiece, showing the incredible skill of the ancient Egyptian craftsman. Not only is the construction complex, but it is the right construction for an object designed to be used for a specific purpose and liable to be subjected to great stress and strain when in use.

This volume is an attempt to bring together information on all aspects of transport in Ancient Egypt, with particular emphasis on the actual surviving examples.

I would like to take this opportunity to thank those who have helped me with this task: Peter Phillips, for his help in taking the photographs, proof-reading and for his invaluable assistance and support; Dave Montford, who developed and printed all my photographs; Peter Robinson, for producing the maps and hieroglyphs used in the text; Anthea Page, Juanita Homan and Robin Page, who are *The Rubicon Press*, for their support and encouragement.

INTRODUCTION

A good communications system is essential for any community, culture or civilisation to flourish. Without the means, and of course the will to communicate, some of the great civilisations of the Ancient World would not have arisen.

This is particularly so in the case of Egypt, which in prehistoric times consisted of many separate villages and communities spread along the length of the river Nile. It was the unique geography and topography of the country which enabled these communities to make contact with their neighbours. Some of this contact may not necessarily have been welcome, for not only were friendly exchanges possible, but aggressive communities were able to oppress and subdue their neighbours.

A mixture of this friendly grouping together of communities for their mutual benefit and enforced grouping following acts of aggression combined to bring these separate communities together into two Kingdoms of Upper and Lower Egypt. Around 3100 B.C. these two Kingdoms were united under one Pharaoh.

The civilisation of Ancient Egypt flourished for the next three thousand years with periods of greatness alternating with periods of depression, conflict and turmoil. Following times when the unification of the country faltered, the country's excellent communication network was easily re-established by the stronger Pharaohs. This network, centred around transport on the river and roads came to support a vast empire, which, at its height, stretched around the eastern end of the Mediterranean Sea and south to Nubia.

The unique climate of Egypt, together with the funeral beliefs, has meant that actual examples of various methods of transport have survived. Special emphasis is given in this volume to these examples, which are examined in some detail, together with the story of their discovery, excavation and conservation.

In the following chapters we will examine the types of transport used in Ancient Egypt.

As some technical terms with which the reader may be unfamiliar are included in the text, a glossary of nautical terms and of those relating to chariots is included as an appendix.

The scope of the subject is large and this volume can only provide a broad overview. The bibliography lists other relevant works, should further reading be required.

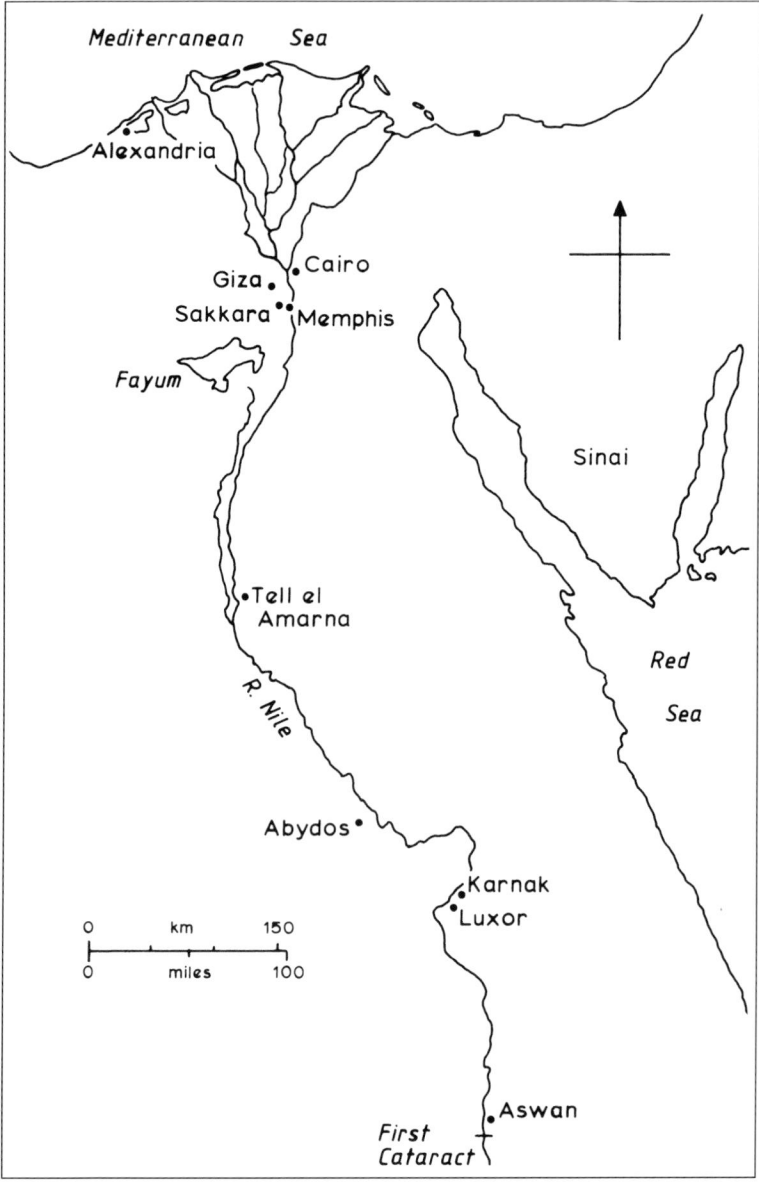

1. *Map of Egypt*

I TRANSPORT ON WATER

Many books on Ancient Egypt begin with an oft-quoted statement made by the Greek historian, Herodotus, around 447 B.C., that Egypt is the "Gift of the River". Cliché it may be, but no one since has really summed up the position quite as succinctly as Herodotus. Quite simply, without the river Nile Egypt would be nothing but an arid desert, where no civilisation could ever have flourished.

The use of the river and boats became one of the main features in the daily lives of the Ancient Egyptians and was also to affect their religious thoughts profoundly.

The river Nile flows northwards from almost the centre of the African continent through Egypt. Four Cataracts interrupt the flow, but from Aswan to the Mediterranean there are no natural obstacles over a distance of some seven hundred and fifty miles.

The First Cataract at Aswan was navigable at times of high water and at low water small boats could be pulled through. Attempts were made to deepen the river at the Cataracts but the larger boats would still have had to be removed from the water and pulled along the river banks to clear the obstruction.

The water from the river supports a relatively narrow band of arable land on either bank in southern Egypt and the large area of the river Delta in the north. This land, with its fertile soil and rich vegetation, enabled the early Egyptians to gather food and produce crops. It supported a variety of wild life which was hunted (and some of which were later domesticated) for food. The river itself teemed with fish. Early sites of habitation are littered with fish bones, which show that full advantage was taken of this readily available food supply.

The fish could be caught from the land by lines, nets or harpoons. Many paintings and reliefs show fishermen at their work. Fish hooks, (virtually identical to those used by anglers around the world today) both barbed and un-barbed, have been found at many Predynastic sites and were used throughout Egypt's long history.

2. *View of the river Nile and the Theban mountains at Luxor*

The early fishermen probably discovered rapidly that the best
fish often lay in the deeper water and that a better catch could be
obtained by venturing out onto the river. Noticing, no doubt, that
reeds floated upon the surface of the water, it did not take long
to realise that a bundle of these reeds tied together could easily
support the weight of a man and provide a platform from which
to fish. Propelled by hands, wooden oars or poles, these small
rafts were probably only used near the river bank and in relatively
still water. Nets and fishing lines could now be dropped directly
into areas of deeper water and catches would have improved.
Larger rafts provided a more stable platform from which the
hunters could use harpoons and spears. Such rafts may well have
made fishing safer as crocodiles were common throughout Egypt
in Dynastic times.

Working singly, or in pairs, fishermen could spread nets from
riverside to boat or between two boats. Hitting the water with a
long pole frightened the fish and drove them towards the nets –
a technique which is still used today.

From small one-man rafts, larger craft soon developed and are
the subject of some of the earliest recognisable paintings from
Ancient Egypt. Depictions of the first boats have been found on
rocks at the early sites and on pottery of the Predynastic Period.
These paintings, and the numbers of them which have survived,
indicate that the use of boats had become widespread throughout the country and that they had developed considerably from
the first simple rafts.

4

3. Modern fishermen on the river Nile at Luxor

Wooden boats also probably developed at an early stage in Egyptian history. Wood has always been a scarce commodity in Egypt, but recent excavations and studies have indicated that in the Prehistoric and possibly the early Dynastic periods, the climate was more favourable. Rain fell in Egypt and areas which are now desert may well have been able to support vegetation, which would have included some trees which were large enough to provide timber for boat building.

Once the idea of river travel had been established with the use of papyrus craft, the development of wooden boats was rapid as the potential of the use of the river as a highway was exploited to the full. Boats could be used to travel from one bank of the river to the other and to travel further afield, both up and downstream.

The current of the river flows northwards and is sufficiently strong to carry vessels downstream at a moderate pace. The river flows at an average speed of 1 knot (1.85 kilometres per hour) and this speed increased to 4 knots when the river was in flood. (With the building of the Aswan High Dam, the river in Egypt no longer floods and the flow of the river is now controlled).

Large oars at the stern of the vessels gave them some "steerage" and enabled them to navigate a more precise course to avoid any obstacles or mud banks in the river. Travelling upstream required great exertion on oars to propel the vessels, but once again the environment provided the main means of power, for the prevailing wind in the country blows upstream (i.e. north to south). The introduction of sails harnessed this power. A boat under sail even became the hieroglyph 🛶 for travelling south, whilst a boat without a sail or mast was the hieroglyph for travelling north 🛶 .

Travel, up and down the country, now became a possibility and, rapidly, a reality. Villages were no longer quite so remote from each other. Contact between different areas (friendly or otherwise) became easier. This factor alone probably played no small part in the early history of Egypt. Once contact had been established, villages became grouped together for their mutual benefit in districts or "nomes" and ultimately into the two separate Kingdoms of Upper and Lower Egypt.

When a King of Upper Egypt (usually identified as King Narmer) conquered Lower Egypt and unified the country around 3100 B.C., he established his capital at Memphis, virtually on the border between the two Kingdoms. He was secure in the knowledge that he could rapidly send his soldiers to the north or the south if any trouble arose. His decrees could be passed quickly to the rest of the country by his officials and, more importantly, he could travel the country himself, to unite the two Kingdoms firmly and lay the foundations of a civilisation which was to last for over three thousand years.

This unifying effect of the river was unique to Egypt and similar results are not seen in any of the other early civilisations.

At various periods of Egypt's greatness, the traffic on the river Nile must have been considerable. Downstream came gold and granite from Nubia, tribute from Africa, including ebony and ivory. Upstream came tribute and imports from other countries, which would have included precious supplies of timber.

There must also have been a great deal of movement of people, animals and produce, up and down and across the river, especially at important and busy cities such as Memphis and Thebes. During the period of the inundation, when the river Nile would burst its banks, the villages would have been cut off from each other by the flood waters covering the fields and the use of small boats would have been essential to daily life.

Trading expeditions were sent out into the Mediterranean and into the Red Sea. The ancient vessels were clearly capable of sea voyages, although the early mariners would probably have hugged the coast and avoided the open seas.

The larger boats were obviously able to carry very heavy loads such as timber and the heaviest of them all, granite from Aswan which was much prized for building and the making of statues. Some of these ships were enormous; special barges were built during the Old Kingdom (2686–2181 B.C.) to transport granite columns and in the New Kingdom (1570–1070 B.C.) to transport massive obelisks and statues. These barges probably took full advantage of the annual flooding of the river, when they could be sailed as close as possible to the temple sites, on the edges of the cultivated area.

Even war-ships were built and records survive of one of the earliest recorded naval battles, fought during the reign of King Ramesses III (1182–1151 B.C.).

All this activity must have supported an enormous army of workers to build the ships, man them and handle the cargoes. There must have been specially built quays and harbours along the length of the river Nile, although few of them have survived. In most cases, the vessels would simply have been moored to the river banks. All vessels carried wood stakes, which could be driven into the bank, and ropes used to secure the bows and stern of the vessel. As most vessels had a shallow draft and a relatively flat bottom, it would not have been too difficult for them to be pulled up onto the banks of the river when necessary.

The temples had special quays in front of them. A canal led from the river to a rectangular basin at the temple entrance for cargo vessels, and the ceremonial barges used to transport the

4. Stone quayside at the entrance to the temple of Amun at Karnak

5. Stone slipway at the entrance to the temple of Karnak

images of the Gods during religious festivals. The quays were also used by the King when he visited the temple. The basin was large enough to enable most boats to be turned around, so that they could enter and leave bow-first.

The original quayside at the temple of Karnak still survives, although the canal to the river and the basin have long been filled in. A high quayside enabled larger highsided vessels to be docked directly at the temple entrance.

In addition to the quayside, a sloping ramp or slipway runs from the river bank down to the original water level, which would have allowed smaller vessels to be pulled directly onto the river bank at the Temple entrance and also to be relaunched easily.

This quayside and slipway at Karnak would not just have been used for people, but for landing the vast amount of building materials used to construct the temple, materials such as granite from Aswan and other fine stones transported by river from the north and the south. During most of the New Kingdom there was continuous and major building work undertaken at the site, so much so, that one wonders how the religious rituals were performed at the heart of what can only be described as a vast building site. At any one time there would have been an almost constant stream of passenger and cargo boats to the quayside, in addition to its use for ceremonial and religious occasions.

At Birket Habu in Thebes, on the west bank of the river Nile,

Amenhotep III (1386–1349 B.C.) had an enormous harbour constructed. This harbour served his palace at Malkata, but probably also served as the landing point for the building materials for his large funerary temple, also on the West Bank. The harbour basin has now filled with silt and wind blown sand, and is barely discernable when visiting the site, although the large mounds of material excavated when the harbour was originally constructed can still be seen. Of the buildings which once surrounded the site, little remains. Only the lower courses of the walls of the mud-brick palace survive and even the huge blocks of stone used to build the funerary temple of the King some kilometres away from Malkata have been removed and re-used elsewhere, leaving only a few shattered blocks and the two colossal statues, known to us today as the Colossi of Memnon. Nothing survives of the vessels which must have used the harbour at Malkata at the height of Egypt's power and prosperity. For evidence of the boats which plied the river, we have to look elsewhere.

(a) The Evidence

Our knowledge of Ancient Egyptian boats comes from a variety of sources, which include clay models and painted pottery dating from 5000 B.C. to 3000 B.C.

From the large number of early representations of boats which have survived, it is clear that water transport was considered an essential part of life in Ancient Egypt from the Predynastic period onwards. Representations of boats became more common in the Dynastic period and are shown in tomb and temple reliefs for the whole of the long history of Egypt.

Whilst there is a great deal of information which can be obtained from the reliefs and paintings, much interpretation of the evidence is required. The scenes and reliefs distort the perspective, or indeed have no perspective at all (as happens with the representation of the human body in Egyptian art). There is also no idea of the scale of the vessels shown. A human figure can be shown next to a boat, but figure and boat can be to a different scale. If we can rely on the accuracy of the artists, in some instances the number of figures shown on board may give some indication of the size of the vessel, but this literal interpretation is fraught with difficulties. The artists simplified many of the details of the craft in their work, when showing, for example, details of the hull, rigging and crew. The vessels are invariably shown floating far higher in the water than they would have been in reality.

Another invaluable source of information is available to us in the form of model boats which have been found in great numbers in tombs. These models, made of wood, plastered and brightly painted, show vessels propelled by oars and sail, which are often equipped with a full complement of sailors. Examples of such models, large and small and of varying quality of workmanship, can be found in most museums which have Egyptian collections.

Tombs contained at least two models, one with a mast and sail and one without. Endowed with magical powers, they would enable the deceased to travel freely in the afterworld. One boat would enable him to sail upstream, using the power of the wind, whilst the second boat would float downstream with the current of the river or be propelled by oars.

During the Middle Kingdom (2040–1782 B.C.) the number of boat models found in some of the wealthier tombs increased. A particularly large collection was discovered by Herbert Winlock in 1920 in the tomb of Meketra, Chancellor to King Mentuhotep III. A total of twelve boats, together with other models which included houses, a butcher's shop and stables, were discovered in a small sealed chamber in the otherwise empty tomb. As many of the models were in pairs, the collection was divided between the Cairo Museum and the Metropolitan Museum in New York.

Relatively few models survive which can be dated to the New Kingdom (1570–1070 B.C.). Battered examples were found in some of the plundered royal tombs in the Valley of the Kings, but intact examples of royal model boats were found in the tomb of Tutankhamun, where a veritable fleet of vessels, thirty-five in total, were discovered in 1922 by Howard Carter and Lord Carnarvon.

Once again though, the artists invariably simplified the details of their models. The "sheer" or curve of the hull of the boat is usually over exaggerated. The hull shape is often distorted for another, more practical reason: many vessels are shown with flat bottoms, simply to enable the models to stand upright on the floor of the tomb. Just to add to the confusion, there were actually some flat bottomed vessels, so we have to attempt to differentiate between these and the round-bottomed craft.

Tutankhamun's boats have no figures on board which would help to give some idea of scale, although, where figures are included on other models, the scale of the boat and the figures is often not the same.

The craftsmen who made these splendid models also made mistakes – one model in the British Museum has the bow and the stern reversed!

Despite these problems, there is a wealth of information available from these sources and with a little knowledge of boat building techniques in general, it is possible to make reasonably accurate reconstructions of their actual appearance.

We have, however, one final, invaluable and unique source of information, preserved in Egypt's dry climate for thousands of years... full sized examples of the boats themselves. Few in number, they nevertheless establish the proportions, designs and building techniques, which changed little over the centuries. Details on paintings and models which appear unclear, can now be re-examined and compared with the surviving examples of the vessels. More examples may be discovered in the future which may help to clarify some areas where the existing evidence is unclear or non existent. In the meantime, taking all the sources of information into account, the vessels of the Dynastic Period of Ancient Egypt can be reconstructed with reasonable accuracy.

They are of two distinct types: firstly the papyrus vessels, made from bundles of reeds tied together, the earliest craft to sail on the river, and secondly, the wooden vessels. The wooden boats themselves can be divided into two groups. The first group resemble the shapes of the original papyrus craft. They are known as "papyriform" craft and were primarily used for religious and funerary purposes. The second group were the "working" craft which carried cargoes and passengers, and were of a different, more practical design.

(b) Papyrus Boats

Boats made of papyrus reeds were probably the first to sail on the river. The actual reed used is generally assumed to be papyrus, rather than any other species of reed which may have grown on the banks of the river Nile. "Cyperus Papyrus", to give it its full name, can grow up to five metres in height and up to fifteen centimetres thick at the base of each stem. Whilst papyrus no longer grows in Egypt, because of climatic changes over the last two thousand years, in the earliest periods it grew along the length of the river, although by the time of the New Kingdom (1570 B.C.) it was found only in the Delta. Today it does not survive in the wild in Egypt and only grows in one or two areas where it has deliberately been re-introduced in modern times.

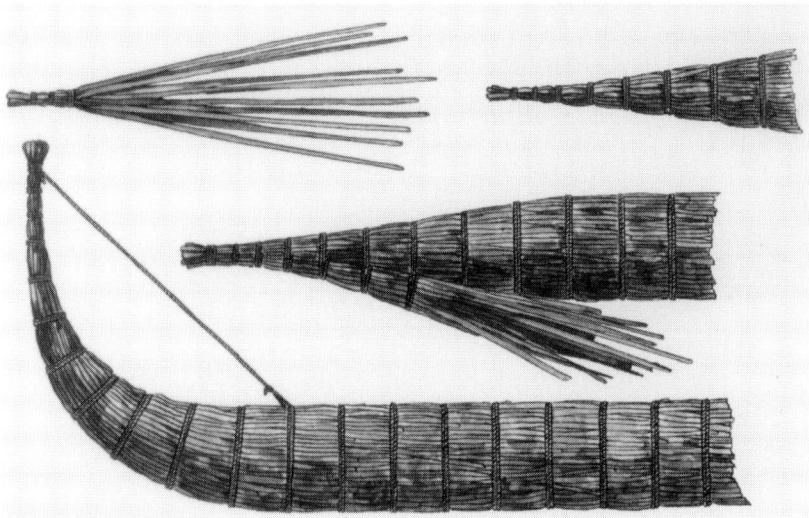

6. The method of construction of a papyrus boat

Papyrus reeds are very pliable, but not particularly durable (unless they remain dry, as, for example, when made into the "paper" of the Ancient Egyptians, which has survived in large quantities). Paintings depicting papyrus craft and painted wooden models show the papyrus as green in colour, which indicates that fresh reeds were used, rather than reeds which had been dried first. The green colour may simply be an artistic convention, but such conventions usually have some solid foundation. (A similar example of an artistic convention based on reality is that representations of the male figure are usually painted a darker colour than female figures, because the men were exposed to the sun and were actually darker in colour than the women).

Papyrus reed boats are still made and used in the Lake Chad area of Africa, where dried stalks are preferred to freshly cut reeds. Explorer and traveller Thor Heyerdal used dried papyrus reeds to construct his two boats *Ra I* and *Ra II*, which both sailed the Atlantic ocean in 1969 and 1970 A.D.. Whilst it may be questionable whether Heyerdal proved there actually was any direct contact between the "new" and the "old" world, he did at least prove that papyrus craft were potentially capable of sea journeys.

Ra I and *Ra II* were both approximately 13.7 metres long, 4.6 metres wide and 1.8 metres deep. Both boats carried a crew of seven men plus all their equipment and supplies needed for the long voyage. *Ra I*, however, never completed the long journey across the Atlantic and foundered mid-way. *Ra II* stayed afloat for some fifty-seven days and completed the crossing. After all this time in the water though, the reeds used in her construction had become heavily water-logged, and she would probably not have been able to stay afloat for much longer.

It is generally considered that fresh papyrus reeds would be less durable than those which had been dried before use, but it would be an interesting experiment to compare the long-term floating qualities of fresh and dried papyrus. If green papyrus floats, it is likely to absorb less additional water than would dried papyrus and, therefore, might stay afloat for a longer period. Fresh or dried, it is obvious that papyrus has a limited life as a boat-building material and this perhaps indicates that few, if any, large vessels would have been constructed of papyrus, when the amount of labour is weighed against the actual working life of the completed craft. If Thor Heyerdal's experiment and experience with his papyrus ships is representative, and papyrus lasts as long in fresh water as in salt water, a working life of only two months could have been expected.

Egyptologist Flinders Petrie believed that the reed vessels were painted with pitch to stop them from getting waterlogged, which would have extended their working life. Whilst this would have been possible and perhaps practical, there is no actual evidence, either from surviving boats or from paintings and reliefs of such vessels, to prove this theory.

Most of the earliest craft were probably relatively small. Larger craft may have been constructed for religious or funerary purposes, where an extended working life would not be required.

The papyrus boats are essentially rafts, the sides of the vessels being without any enclosing gunwales. They were made from cut reeds, tied together with rope into bundles. Small bundles were joined with other small bundles, and by introducing more reeds into the bundles as they were lengthened, they became wider forming the tapering bow shape.

Once the required width of the boat was achieved, the number of reeds in the bundles was then reduced, forming the tapered stern. Several bundles of reeds would be tied together and the slender, tapering bow and stern would be raised upwards, often at right angles to the water, giving these vessels the distinctive shape seen in the representations painted on the earliest pottery. Additional bundles tied along the sides of the hull, at water level, helped to make the vessel more stable and give it a more distinctive boat shape. (See *fig 6.*)

The triangular cross-section of the papyrus stems meant that, when tied tightly together, they formed a very compact and strong bundle with few air spaces or gaps between the stems.

Some of the earliest recognisable representations of boats are clay models which date to the Badarian Culture (around 5500–4000 B.C.).

These models show small boats which are presumed to be representations of papyrus boats as there is no evidence from this very early period of the necessary woodworking skills needed to

7. *Pottery model of a boat, c.5000 B.C. from El Badari*

8. Decorated Predynastic pot from the Nagada II Period (left) 9. Decorated Predynastic pot from the Nagada II Period, showing a boat with a sail (right)

build wooden boats. The built-up sides of these early models do look as if they represent dug-out canoes, but this is considered unlikely as there is no native timber in Egypt of sufficient size and quality to build such boats, which require a large, single log. Only future discoveries will remove this uncertainty.

In the Amratian/Nagada I period (4000–3500 B.C.) painted pottery is found which clearly shows vessels of some kind. Again, these are presumed to be papyrus boats. On later painted pottery from the Nagada II Period (3500–3000 B.C.) the paintings clearly show the papyrus bundles from which the vessels were constructed.

The painted pottery depictions show vessels with upswept bows and sterns, which narrow to a point. This is typical of papyrus craft.

From the Nagada II Period, some vessels are shown which do not have the pointed bows and sterns. Blunt-ended, these may show wooden vessels. We know from the archaeological evidence that woodworking tools were available at this time and various cut wooden planks have been found in tombs.

The illustrations on the pots are highly stylised, but help to show how the simple raft has evolved.

The drawings, executed in simple brush-strokes using a red-ochre pigment, show what is presumed to be oars along the sides of the boats, (although if they are oars, the artists invariably show far more than would have been practical or possible). These lines may just be the artist's way of trying to show the ripples on the water or the reflection of the boat. In many cases these lines only start at the water level, not from the deck level as would be expected if oars were being represented. The lines of the oars would also cross the hull of the boat, which these lines do not.

Larger steering oars are shown at the stern of the vessels and cabins are shown amidships. Some drawings may show a simple mast and a sail, but the details are invariably unclear. Other drawings appear to show branches from a palm tree (or possibly a whole tree) at the bows. This may have been an early attempt by the boatbuilders to harness the power of the wind. The wind against the palm would provide better steerage and possibly add some actual speed to the vessel. Many of the elements of these early drawings are obscure and their real meanings are open to interpretation.

Models of early boats also survive. These are assumed to be of papyrus craft, as the bundles of tied reeds are clearly indicated. All the known Predynastic models show flat-bottoms only, whereas after this period rounded bottoms are seen. As has already been stated it is not wise to place too much emphasis on such evidence, for it may be the artistic convention or the limited skills of the model makers.

Some representations clearly show a mask or some decoration at the bows, although the exact form and reason is not known. Another odd feature is often a tassel-shaped object, shown hanging beneath the bows. This has variously been interpreted as an anchor or a fender, with the latter usually being considered more likely. Fenders are, however, only really needed to protect the sides of vessels when moored against quaysides. Most boats would have been moored to the sloping banks of the river, which

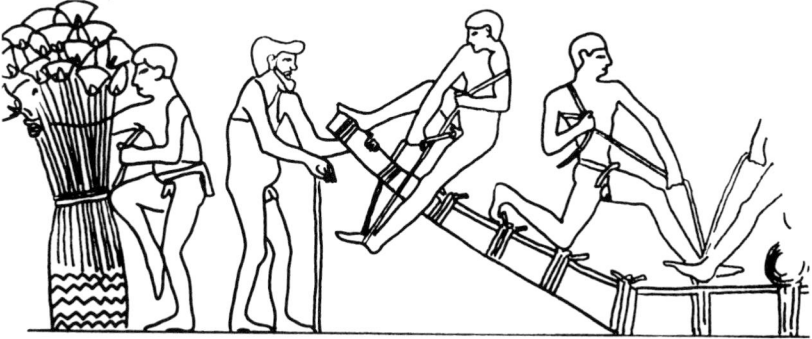

10. Old Kingdom scene of the making of a papyrus boat, from Meir

11. Reconstruction of a papyrus boat

would also negate the need for an anchor. It is possible that these odd objects are simply weights attached to a line, used to establish the depth of the water, a necessary task when navigating a river full of constantly shifting mud banks. The tassled effect may be the artist trying to show water running from the weight (possibly a stone) when it is pulled clear of the water. Whilst we are familiar with the conventions of the Egyptian artists of the Dynastic Period, these early artists were not working with such conventions and were trying to represent what they saw.

Tomb scenes from the Old Kingdom show the making of papyrus boats (although the boats are always shown virtually completed, omitting the early stages of construction). The boat builders are shown cutting the papyrus reeds and then tightening the ropes on the hull of the boat. In the scene reproduced here (*fig 10*) an older man with a walking stick stands at the bow. He is probably the experienced boat builder and is directing the operation. No manuals survive from Ancient Egypt on "how to

12. Model showing papyrus fishing boats from the tomb of Meketra

build a boat" and, like many manual and artistic skills, the techniques would have been passed from father to son through the generations.

The drawing of a reconstructed papyrus boat shows the method of construction and the characteristic shape of such craft. An attempt has been made to show how such a vessel would look in the water. The original craft dates to around 3200 B.C.. The high bow and stern needed to be held in place by a rope, running from the tip to the body of the boat. This would help to keep the shape and also prevent sagging in the water, a problem experienced by Thor Heyerdal with his papyrus boats *Ra I* and *Ra II*. Sagging bows and sterns cause boats to wallow in the water and make them very difficult to steer.

The bow of the vessel is on the right of the illustration, with the bundles of reeds tied in a vertical position, whilst the stern has the bundles pulled from the vertical towards the bow. Exactly why the bow and stern of the vessels was made in this way is not known, but this form was used for papyriform boats for the next

13. Painting from the New Kingdom tomb of Nebamun, showing Nebamun hunting wildfowl in the marshes

19

14. *Gilt figure of Tutankhamun harpooning from a papyrus raft*

three thousand years. Steering is by means of a large oar placed at the stern. The boat was propelled by either oars or sail. The sail shown in this reconstruction is made of fibre matting tied to a top and bottom yard-arm. A small cabin on the deck, which would have provided some shelter for the crew or passengers, is made of a rough timber framework and covered with matting.

Because of the flimsy nature of the construction material it is likely that these vessels did not achieve a great size. An overall length of seventeen metres is generally assumed, from later evidence and representations, to have been the maximum. This would have allowed ten or twelve oars per side, with a gap of about a metre between each oar position.

Although the reconstruction shows a single mast, it is believed that the masts on these early papyrus craft may have been bipod, i.e. a double mast, rather like an "A"-shaped ladder. This type of mast would have been easier to fix to the relatively flimsy and flexible hull than a single mast. Bipod masts are also seen frequently in the many later Middle Kingdom wooden boat models. Most of the early representations appear to show only single masts, but this may well be one of the over-simplifications on the part of the artists, for if seen from the side, a bipod mast looks the same as a single mast.

With the introduction of wood as a building material, the use of papyrus appears to have been discontinued for major vessels, but probably continued to be used by fishermen and hunters. A major consideration would have been the easy availability of papyrus compared with the expensive imported wood.

Middle Kingdom models from the tomb of Meketra in the Cairo Museum clearly show two papyrus boats towing a fishing net between them. The boats are painted green and the ropes holding the papyrus bundles together are clearly shown. Small papyrus boats and rafts are depicted in the tombs of the nobles at Thebes, which date to the New Kingdom.

Small rafts could support the weight of one or two people. Their decks were reinforced with wood, which can usually be clearly seen in the paintings. These small craft were used as floating platforms when hunting wildfowl in the marshes. They were probably reasonably stable in such a situation, where they were used in relatively shallow water and surrounded by growing reeds which would have given them additional support. It is unlikely that they would have been very stable or of much practical use in more open water. These simple craft appear in

15. Detail of the papyrus raft from the painting from the tomb of Nebamun

representations throughout Egypt's long history and were used by rich and poor alike.

Two statuettes from the tomb of Tutankhamun, one of which is shown here, depict the King, balanced on a small papyrus raft, in the act of throwing a harpoon (probably aimed at a hippopotamus). In practice, such a narrow raft, as depicted, is unlikely to have been able to support the weight of a man and it would have needed to have been wider to provide a stable platform from which to hunt. Artistic convention has here reduced the size of the raft to more elegant proportions. On the other hand, the skills required to use such rafts would be similar to those required by the users of modern sailboards who are able to balance successfully on them even when they are stationary. The dimensions and shape of these two craft, separated by thousands of years of human technological development, would appear to be remarkably similar.

Plutarch, writing at the end of Egypt's long history, recounted the myth of the Goddess Isis who used a papyrus raft when searching for the body of her dead husband, Osiris. Plutarch stated that the Egyptians believed that papyrus rafts were never attacked by crocodiles. In ancient times, crocodiles were a real

22

threat on the river. This belief was undoubtedly based on fact, for crocodiles are attracted by movement in the water and would pay far more attention to a human moving about in the water than to something floating on the surface. In fact they would probably show little, if any, reaction to a papyrus craft drifting by them on the river, especially if the crew were cautious in their movements. This may be why papyrus boats and papyriform craft were considered as being special and remained in use for religious and funerary purposes throughout Egypt's long history.

(c) Wooden Boats

In most countries, the first wooden craft ever seen were dug-out canoes, made by hollowing out trunks of trees. This type of craft is unlikely to have been seen in Ancient Egypt as there were little, if any, suitable trees which would provide large enough trunks to be used in this way. We do know that the climate in the country has changed over the centuries, so it is possible that in Prehistoric times there may have been trees which were suitable, but there is no real evidence to confirm or disprove this.

Some of the early models of boats, already mentioned in connection with papyrus boats, do look as if they might represent dug-out canoes, as they have high sides. It is possible that these models do show simple wooden boats, ones not made from a single log, but from planks of wood which were lashed together to form a box-type hull. The planks would have been joined by rope and this type of craft could well have been the ancestor of the more complex wooden boats seen in later periods.

The native Egyptian woods are acacia, sycamore and persea. Acacia is a hard wood and is suitable for boatbuilding. The acacia tree is relatively small, but we know that in ancient times it was difficult to obtain large pieces of timber. Planks of acacia rarely exceed 2.5 metres in length. Whilst some larger trees may have been available in the earliest periods, this is unlikely. Cedar was used in later periods for boat building, but had to be imported, probably from the Lebanon. It was not until trade links had been established with countries outside Egypt, at the beginning of the Old Kingdom, that larger logs became available. Cedar was highly prized and could provide planks in excess of twenty metres in length.

The use of wood on a larger scale and for the construction of more complex hulls had to wait until the technology was available to cut, shape and join the timbers. This involved skilled woodworking techniques and the use of fairly advanced tools. From the evidence of woodworking which survives, these skills were not really available until just before the beginning of the

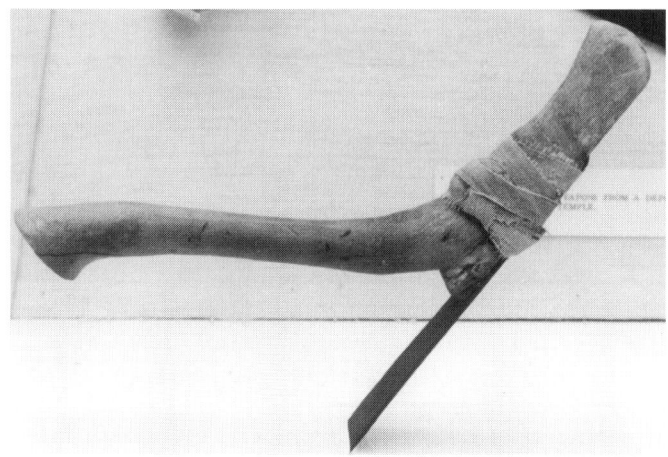

16. Model adze from the foundation deposit of the temple of Thutmose III at Deir el Bahri

Dynastic Period, which is when the use of wood for boat and ship construction probably started.

Copper-bladed adzes, axes, saws and chisels were used by the carpenters and boat builders. These tools were capable of cutting logs into planks and were also used for far more delicate and complicated carpentry techniques. Iron tools were not available until the end of the New Kingdom.

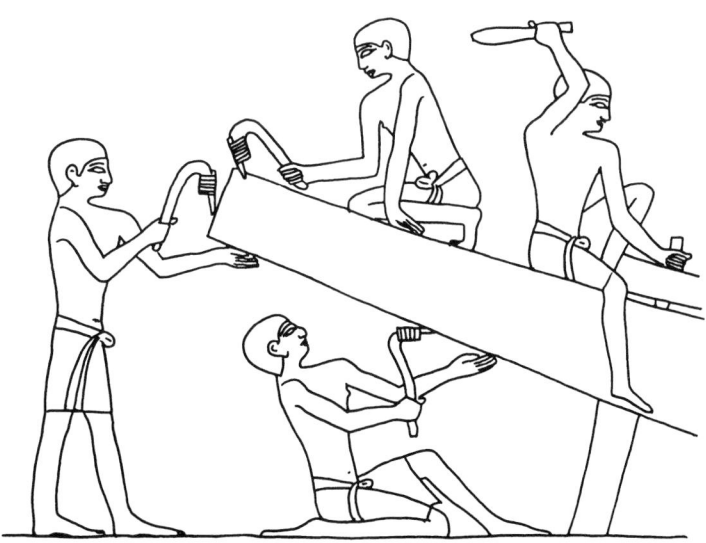

17. Relief from the Old Kingdom tomb of Ti at Sakkara, showing workmen wielding adzes working on a wooden boat

In its simplest form, a wooden boat can consist of a bottom and two sides. The side planks were fixed to the bottom, in the earliest times, by rope made from flax, halfa grass and esparto grass. This type of construction sounds very flimsy, but can prove remarkably effective. When wet, wood expands and the rope shrinks, which provides a watertight seal between the planks.

Many of the early wooden craft are papyriform in shape. This means that the shape of the hull is almost identical to the shape of the papyrus craft. It is difficult to know why the construction of wooden craft followed the shape of the papyrus vessels. To some extent, the similarity in shape may be coincidental, in that boats tend to be made in similar "boat" shapes the world over, with no obvious connection between the builders. Perhaps a comparison can be made with the evolution of architectural design, where the features of mud-brick buildings were reproduced almost exactly in stone, when this medium was first used. The builders followed designs and shapes with which they were readily familiar, and this may well have been the case with the boat-builders.

The decorated bows and sterns of the wooden vessels imitated the tied bundles of papyrus, although the features became more stylised. The first boat builders in wood even reproduced the appearance of the rope used to tie the original papyrus bundles together.

It is usually assumed that the papyriform vessels were the ones used for religious or funerary purposes and for royal burials. In representations of the boats used to carry the gods across the heavens, it is papyriform vessels which are shown. The early beliefs were probably established at the time when it was only papyrus craft which were seen on the Nile.

Many boat graves have been found in Egypt, although most are empty. The earliest dates to the reign of Hor Aha (around 3050 B.C.). W.B. Emery discovered a boat burial close to the mastaba tomb sometimes attributed to King Hor Aha at Sakkara. The boat was placed in a shallow pit situated to the north of the tomb and covered with a mud brick superstructure which followed the outline of the boat. Fragments of wood and rope in the pit were taken as evidence that it had once contained a boat.

Another tomb at Sakkara, number 3506, also discovered by Emery, once contained a full sized boat. Little remains of the boat, but the evidence, which included impressions in the sand and fragments of timber, indicated a large vessel some fourteen and a half metres in length. Unfortunately, not enough information remained to enable the archaeologists to determine the details of the construction of the boat as no large identifiable fragments of timber survived. The boat had been laid in a shallow depression and propped upright with blocks of wood. Mud brick walls surrounded the boat which would have been covered with sand. A final layer of mud bricks covered the resultant boat-shaped mound.

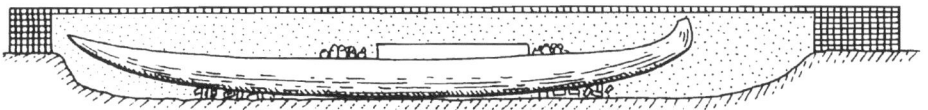

18. Reconstruction of a boat burial from the Archaic Period. Tomb 3506 at Sakkara

Other boat burials from this period at Helwan, on the east bank of the river Nile opposite Sakkara, can be connected with the burials of nobles, but from the Old Kingdom onwards almost all boat burials are found connected with Royal burials only. In later periods the practice of the burial of full sized boats was discontinued and models ritually and magically replaced the full sized vessels.

The only identifiable pieces of timber from an early wooden boat were found at Tarkhan, south of Cairo. Some planks had been used as part of a coffin, or possibly as roofing material, but they appear to have been used before as part of a boat. Holes in the planks indicate where ropes may have been used to lash the planks together. These fragments are now in the Petrie Museum of Egyptology, University College, London.

Until recently, no complete examples of any of the early boats had been found, but a recent discovery of what would appear to be a fleet of boats has been made at Abydos. These were found near the funerary enclosure of King Khasekhemwy of the Second Dynasty and clearly belong to one of the nearby First Dynasty enclosures.

Dating to the early centuries of the third millennium B.C. twelve mounds have been found, from eighteen to twenty-one metres long, each one containing a boat. It would appear that, as with the boat burials at Sakkara, a shallow trench was dug and the boat laid in it. Most of the hulls remained above ground level and were then surrounded by and filled with mud bricks, producing tombs similar to those found by Emery at Sakkara. The resultant white-painted mounds retained the distinctive boat shape.

The remains of these early boat burials were found by David O'Connor in 1991, during an excavation at the site under the aegis of the University of Pennsylvania Museum of Archaeology and Yale University.

Excavation and examination of these boats has yet to be completed and the exact nature of the find is, at the moment, unclear. That the mounds do contain complete boats is certain, for where the mounds have eroded, the wood of the hulls can clearly be seen. The large size of the mounds indicates that the boats are functional rather than being models.

It is not known as yet for which First Dynasty King these boats were buried, or, indeed if all the boats were buried at the same time and were intended for the same king. The large number of boats at the same location may indicate that they are not meant to represent the morning and evening barges of the Sun God Ra and it is possible that they were used to convey the body and funerary equipment of a dead king to his final resting place and as such, could not be used again.

This find promises to reveal a wealth of information about early boat-building techniques and the results of further excavation at the site are eagerly awaited.

No boat burials have been discovered associated with the early Old Kingdom pyramids at Sakkara, Meidum and Dahshur. This

19. A boat pit by the Great Pyramid of Khufu at Giza

does not mean that boat burials were not made at these sites, for at Meidum and Dahshur in particular, the excavation of the pyramid complexes has not been extensive, and new discoveries may await future archaeologists.

The earliest actual example of a large papyriform wooden boat was discovered in a pit adjacent to the Great Pyramid of Khufu, Pharaoh of the Fourth Dynasty (2589–2566 B.C.) at Giza.

Khufu's Boat

The Great Pyramid of Khufu at Giza is one of the most visited buildings in Egypt. The complex of buildings which surrounded it and the two other Fourth Dynasty pyramids at the same site have been extensively studied and excavated over the last two hundred years. It is, therefore, surprising that new discoveries are still being made at the site today.

The Great Pyramid was once completely surrounded by a boundary wall, which included the subsidiary pyramids. The southern section was built much closer to the pyramid face than the northern or western walls and it was this anomaly which first attracted the attention of an Egyptian architect, Kamal el Mallakh in the early 1950's.

Mallakh was fascinated by the boat pits which surrounded the Giza Pyramids. Five of these pits were discovered near the mortuary temple of Khafra along with a sixth, possibly unfinished pit. The three empty boat pits around the pyramid of Khufu had long been visible. Mallakh was of the opinion that the boundary wall might conceal further pits and that the wall may have been built over them deliberately.

It took him some time to convince the authorities that some preliminary excavation should be undertaken. When the wall was removed, massive stone slabs were found, covering two pits. A cartouche written on one of the blocks gave the name of Djedefre, son and heir of Khufu and the Pharaoh who would have been responsible for the burial of his father. The authorities still needed further convincing that the blocks might cover further boat pits, but eventually permission was given to break through one of the blocks to see what lay underneath.

In 1954, the excavators broke through the block and dis-covered a large cavity below, from which came the distinct smell

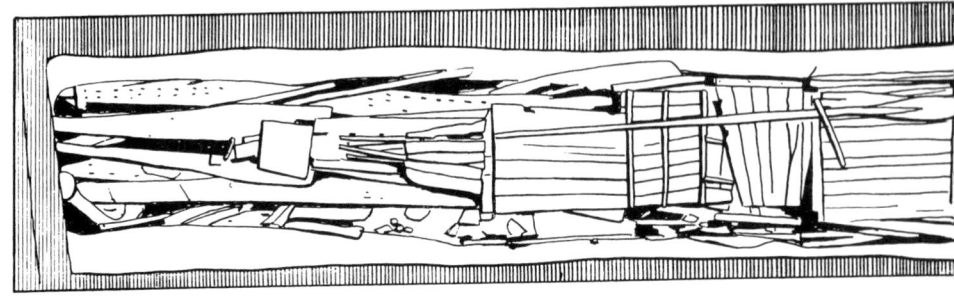

20. *Drawing showing the dismantled boat of Khufu as discovered in the sealed boat pit. The bow*

of wood. By using a mirror, sunlight was reflected into the hole and the light illuminated the blade of an oar, one of the large steering oars of the boat, as it turned out. The contents of this pit appeared to be intact and untouched since the time of Khufu.

Because of the potential problems in the excavation of the boat, which was found to be in pieces, rather than an intact vessel, various committees were formed to prepare for the task. Hag Ahmed Youssef Moustafa was appointed as Chief Excavator. He was to prove a key figure in the restoration of the boat and the success of the task is a reflection of his skill and determination. Hag Ahmed was ably qualified for the task, having gained many years' experience in the restoration of wooden objects. He had worked with George Reisner in 1925 on the restoration of the furniture found in the tomb of Queen Hetepheres (also at Giza and not far from the site of the discovery of the boat). He was completely ignorant of boat building, however, and used some of the planning period to acquaint himself with the techniques of modern wooden boatbuilders and to prepare himself for the excavation and restoration.

One of the first steps in the excavation of the boat was to determine the state of the wood, which was soon established to be almost perfect. The blocks with which the pit had been sealed had been fixed in position with plaster which provided an airtight seal. Initially, the wood and the other organic materials buried in the pit would have given off some moisture, but after a while a state of equilibrium would have been reached and the atmosphere in the pit stabilised. The decision to go ahead and attempt a full restoration of the boat was made.

It was a year before the huge sealing blocks over the pit were removed and the contents of the pit could clearly be seen. What was revealed was a mass of timber, from a boat which had been

dismantled. The individual timbers had been stacked neatly in the pit. Some elements were clearly recognisable, such as the oars, the papyrus shaped stem-post and sections of the decking.

Piece by piece, the timbers were removed from the pit, their exact locations being carefully noted to ensure that any clues which might later aid the reconstruction would not be missed. There were thirteen clear layers of timber. The contents of the pit had been placed there in some order and some timbers had been neatly tied in bundles. These bundles of timbers were presumed to have come from the same sections of the boat. The largest pieces of timber, the planks of the hull itself, were found at the bottom of the pit. It was noticed that some of the timbers bore carpenter's marks, which helped the ancient builders to assemble the boat correctly and were also to help the excavators in the restoration.

Remains of quantities of rope were found in the pit and also some larger objects made of matting and cordage, which may well have been the original fenders, used to stop the sides of the boat rubbing against the quayside.

Carbon dating of a piece of rope gave a date of around 2040 B.C., although the Fourth Dynasty is generally placed earlier at around 2600 B.C.. Some variance in dating results are inevitable and further samples would need to be taken to confirm the accuracy of this original dating.

When all the timbers had been removed, they were examined in detail. Most, as expected, were in excellent condition, but some which had lain at the bottom of the pit and had been subjected to the weight of other timbers lying on top of them, were found to be damaged. To enable the restoration to go ahead, these pieces were repaired, reinforced and patched with new pieces of wood, where the extent of the decay made the re-using of the original pieces in the restoration difficult. In a few

21. Composite view of the reconstructed boat of Khufu

cases, some completely new pieces were needed. The main principle adopted was to remove as little of the original wood as possible and to use new pieces only when absolutely necessary.

Cracks and splits in the original timbers were treated and filled with special glue and the surface painted with a grain pattern to disguise the filling and match the colour of the surrounding timbers. All the original timbers were preserved by the application of Polymerised Polyvinyl Acetate (PVA). The PVA was painted onto the timbers with brushes. This treatment was repeated once a year for three years and then every two years following excavation. The PVA seals the wood, locking in the surviving natural moisture and stopping further shrinkage to a large extent. The process is reversible and the PVA had to be removed temporarily from timbers which needed to be bent back into their original shape. Whilst there may have been some logic to the way the timbers were stored in the pit which would have helped an ancient Egyptian boatbuilder, there was insufficient information to make the restoration easy. No other comparable find had ever been made in Egypt and the excavators had no previous experience to guide them.

Hundreds of scale drawings were made of all the pieces and also scale models of the individual timbers. Gradually some idea of the nature of construction was revealed. The excavators were faced with an enormous three-dimensional jig-saw, whose unique pieces, whilst in good condition, were fragile because of their age.

There were to be many false starts in the restoration and many dead ends. In all, five different attempts at restoration were made, until the construction method and the placing of the timbers was certain. The boat was then taken apart and re-assembled several more times before she came to her final resting place in the new museum, built over the pit which had contained the dismantled parts.

The planks which were once curved to the shape of the hull, had been flattened in the pit and had to be coaxed back into shape. To rebend the smaller pieces, clamps were used. Boiling water was liberally poured over the wood and the process repeated several times an hour over a period of many days. The pressure of the clamps was gradually increased until the

22. Scene from an Old Kingdom tomb, showing the bending of the timbers

23. The reconstructed boat of Khufu

timbers had assumed their correct shape. Once this was achieved
the wood was allowed to dry out again naturally, and the shape
was fixed.

The larger timbers presented more of a problem, but once
again they were soaked in boiling water. These timbers were too
large for the use of clamps, so they were lashed to upright posts
set in the ground and pressure was applied with the use of other
ropes, which were gradually tightened. Some of the planks, in

24. *View of the port side of the boat of Khufu*

addition to being flattened, were also twisted and this too had to be corrected. The correction treatment was brutal and it is a miracle that the ancient timbers survived it and the stresses on the timbers caused by the rebuilding and dismantling of the boat. The timbers had to be man-handled into position and even be able to support the weight of the men involved in the rebuilding, who had to work on the ancient hull and deck timbers.

In ancient times, the timbers would have been bent into position by placing a forked post on the bottom of the boat and fastening ropes to the end of the timbers to be bent. The ropes would have been placed over the fork of the post and the ropes twisted to tighten them. One Old Kingdom scene from a tomb at Zawiyet el Mateiyn shows this process. (See *fig 22.*)

The workmen are shown trimming and fixing the timbers into place and also carving a block of timber at the bow into a figurehead, possibly a hedgehog, as is often seen on smaller boats of this period. The timbers, being fresh, would have bent easily, but may have been soaked in water first to make the task easier.

The restored boat of Khufu is large by any standards, with a length of 43.63 metres and a width of 5.66 metres. Her displacement in the water would have been around forty tons. As a comparison, the keel length of H.M.S. *Victory*, Nelson's flagship at the battle of Trafalgar in 1805 A.D., is 45.7 metres.

The boat is built of cedar planks, some fourteen centimetres in thickness. The hull is elegantly papyriform and is formed around

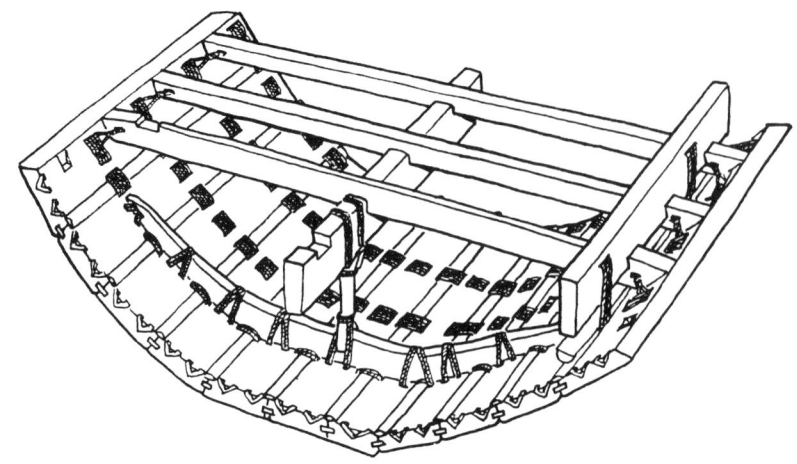

25. Detail of the internal structure of the boat of Khufu

a central plank rather than a conventional keel, a fact which, initially, greatly confused the restorers, who had expected the construction to be similar to large wooden vessels of today.

Positioning the large bottom planks was relatively easy and once in place, the correct location of adjoining timbers could be established by lining up the holes through which passed the ropes used to lash the hull together.

The planks were held together during the reconstruction process by wood supports. When the entire planking sequence had been established, it was possible to estimate how much rope would be needed to finally tie the hull together. In the final restoration a total of five thousand metres of linen rope was used.

The planks are held, or "sewn", together with the rope passing through slots cut into the timbers. The internal strength is provided by ribs and deck beams running across the hull. These strengthening pieces were added to the hull after it had been put together, not built up first before the hull was built up around them, as in most boat construction. Long planks are joined end-to-end using scarf joints, which are secured with rope.

The use of rope to hold the timbers of the hull together may appear to be a flimsy method of construction, but when in water, the wood would have swollen and the ropes shrunk, which would tighten up the hull, giving it great rigidity and making the seams watertight. Wooden battens placed over the seams and lashed into place also served to make the joints tighter and reduce the likelihood of leakage. It is possible that when in use, the seams would be packed (caulked) with papyrus or rope fibres to prevent any seepage, but no evidence of this was found with the boat. The wood of the hull does show, in places, clear impressions of the rope which held it together. This can only have happened when the timbers were wet and is taken as the main evidence that the ship was actually used.

The boat has no mast or sail and was propelled by twelve oars. It is not clear how the oars were used, as there is no evidence of any method of securing the oars to the side of the hull, although rope would probably have been used for this purpose. The oars are also extremely heavy and would have needed more than one man to each oar. It is also uncertain if the rowers stood or were seated. No seats were found, but the oarsmen could have been provided with low benches, which were not included in the pit. The way the oars are displayed on the reconstructed vessel, tied to the framework of the canopy covering the main deck, is for display only and is not intended to represent the manner in which they may have been used. It is possible that, if actually used, the boat would have been towed by a number of smaller craft.

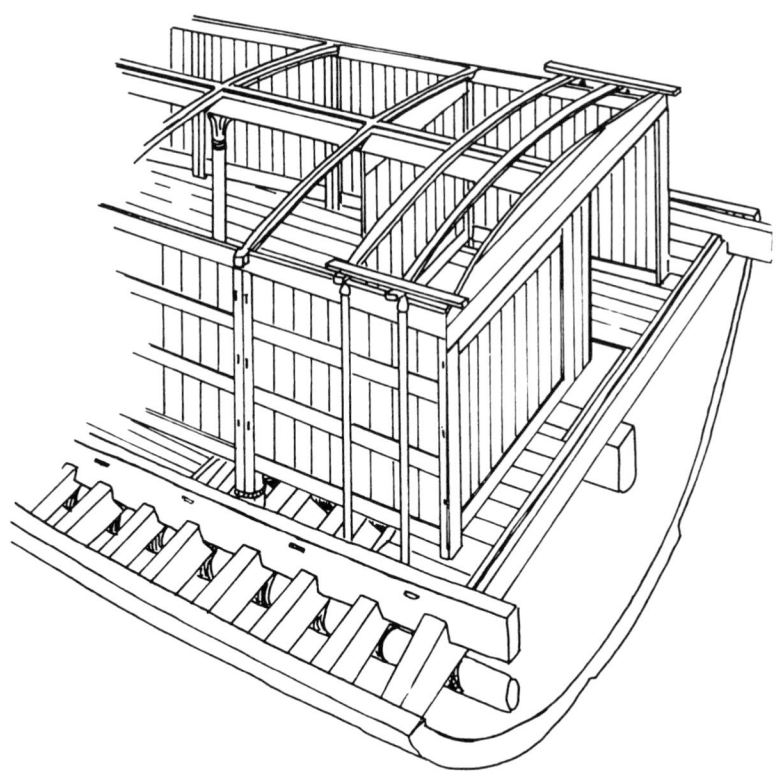

26. Detail of the cabin and canopy of the boat of Khufu

The boat was steered by two larger oars at the stern, one on either side of the vessel. One of the steering oars mounted on the boat today is a replacement as the original was too damaged to use. It is difficult to see how these huge oars were actually used as a tiller (a short pole fixed into the shaft of the oar at a right-angle which would be used to turn the blade of the oar in the water) was never fitted. Perhaps this is another indication that the boat was intended to be towed and manoeuvred by other vessels.

On the deck, near the bows, is a small wooden "baldachin" or canopy. This would have provided some shelter from the sun for any lookouts at the bow of the ship. The role of such a lookout was important in that he would watch out for sandbanks in the river or other obstructions such as floating objects which might damage the vessel. Hippopotami could present as much of a hazard to navigation as sandbanks. The baldachin structure was the first piece of the boat to be recognised as a complete unit when the dismantled timbers were removed from the pit and it was the first to be restored. This canopy could also be used by any

27. Detail of the exterior of the cabin of the boat of Khufu

passengers who wished to sit on the deck rather than in the enclosed cabin.

A framework of wooden poles, forty-eight in total, with papyrus bud capitals, surrounds the large central cabin. These poles would have been covered with matting or thick linen which provided an extra skin to keep the cabin cool in the heat of the sun. This covering may have been brightly painted or decorated in the manner of examples seen in paintings and models. No positive traces of the canopy were found, but the badly decayed remains of several layers of reed mats found in the pit may have served this purpose. Additional supports for a canopy which run along the hull towards the bow would have enabled the main deck area to be covered, and have offered some protection to the crew of the vessel. The wooden canopy supports which cover the deck of the ship are too widely spaced to support a matting canopy, so perhaps a lighter material was used here.

The windowless wooden cabin has two chambers inside, and would have offered some privacy for its occupant. It has a curved roof, and when covered with the second skin of the canopy, it would have been well insulated against the heat. The roof of the larger chamber is supported by two carefully carved central pillars with date palm capitals. One doorway, on the port side of the cabin, leads from the main deck into a small outer chamber. A doorway on the starboard side of this chamber leads into the large main chamber. A third doorway opens from the rear of the large chamber onto the small deck at the stern of the boat. These doorways are not fitted with doors and may have been closed by matting or linen curtains.

This staggered arrangement of doorways means that it is not possible to look from the main deck directly into the main chamber of the cabin.

The cabin has no opening other than the doors and Hag Ahmed reasoned that the matting canopy would have been kept wet to cool the otherwise unventilated interior.

The high stem and stern posts are carved to imitate tied bundles of papyrus. Both are purely ornamental and are made to fit over the end timbers of the bow and stern. The boat could be used without these decorative features which may have been reserved for special occasions.

It is not known if the boat was originally painted. Almost all contemporary illustrations show the hulls of such vessels painted green and yellow, with additional decoration on the cabins and

28. An oar blade from the boat of Khufu

oars. It is odd that no trace of any painted decoration survives on an otherwise well-preserved vessel. Whilst paint may well have worn or washed off some areas of the structure, there would have been many places where one would expect paint to survive, had the boat originally been painted. The assumption must be that the boat was never painted and, therefore, may never have actually been completely finished by the builders.

A wooden gangplank and a stake, to which the boat could be moored at the riverside, were also included in the contents of the pit. The gangplank is very short and could only have been used when the boat was moored by a quayside which was the same level as the deck of the boat.

The exact use of this boat remains a matter of conjecture. It may have been a boat which the King used in life and would need in his afterlife. It may have been made for him to sail the heavens as a God, or it may have been one of the vessels used for the funeral, which meant that it was ritually unable to be used for any other purpose and had to be buried near the King whose body it had carried.

Two points were made by Paul Lipke in his book on the boat of Khufu, in connection with the possible use of the boat.

Firstly, no tests were made at the time of the discovery to see if there were any traces of the remains of microscopic marine life on the timbers below the waterline. This would have proved conclusively whether the boat had ever sailed the river. Tests on a second boat discovered at the site may provide some answers. Secondly, as wood was a scarce commodity, it was usual for timber to be reused, perhaps from previous vessels. In fact such pieces could be considerably older than the "new" vessel. The evidence of the rope marks on some timbers is, therefore, inconclusive evidence that the boat was used, since these marked timbers may have come from an earlier vessel which had been used on the river.

In 1995 a seven-foot wooden model of the boat was made and was tested in a water tank in New York. The intention of Egyptologist Dr. Bob Brier, of Long Island University, was to test the floating characteristics of the boat. The most notable result, which surprised most naval architects and archaeologists, was that the boat, when pulled through the water under different conditions, left very little wake behind it.

Principal dimensions of the boat:

Overall length	43.63 metres
Maximum beam	5.66 metres
Draft	1.48 metres
Total dead weight	150 tons
Cabin:	
Length	9 metres
Small chamber length	2.22 metres
Large chamber length	6.78 metres
Maximum height	2.50 metres
Width fore	4.14 metres
Width aft	2.42 metres
Length of steering oars	6.81 metres
	6.87 metres
Length of oars	from 6.58 to 8.35 metres.

The second sealed pit at the site remained intact and it was not until 1987 that an investigation of it was made by the Egyptian Antiquities Organisation working with the National Geographic Society. One of the main aims of this investigation (as well as ascertaining whether the pit did contain another boat) was to sample the ancient air in the pit and to compare it with the quality of air today. As the first pit was found to be airtight, it was supposed the second would be also.

A hole was bored through the sealing blocks, using equipment which would preserve the air-tight seal. It was also designed to allow a camera and a light to be inserted into the pit to view the contents.

Pressure gauges soon showed that the pit was not hermetically sealed as had been hoped. A disturbing fact was also discovered - that the carbon dioxide level was twice that of the air above ground, which indicated the presence of decaying organic material.

The hopes of the scientists of being able to compare ancient and modern air were dashed, but the cameras did reveal a second dismantled boat.

The camera was able to pick out four oar blades and some panels, possibly from a cabin. This boat appeared to be smaller than the first and one new feature seen was the presence of many copper loops inserted into the wood, presumably used to tie the component parts together. These were not present on the first boat.

It was immediately clear that the timbers were not as well preserved as those of the first boat and that decay had been caused by water seeping into the pit. (This may have occurred relatively recently, for the ground above the pit was used for the mixing of concrete when the museum to house the first boat was being built). A live black beetle was seen on the surface of the timbers which attested to the decay of the organic remains in the pit.

Many Egyptologists believed that the second pit would contain a sailing boat, but no trace was seen of any mast or sails.

The pit was resealed, with no decision, as yet, being made about the excavation of the second boat. One reason for the delay may have been problems experienced with the preservation and restoration of the first boat.

The purpose-built building to house the first boat caused controversy from the day it was built. The internal walkways at three different levels enable excellent views of the hull and deck

29. *Boat pit close to the Great Pyramid of Khufu at Giza, showing the ramp leading down into the pit*

of the boat, but the modern design, literally right against the face of the Great Pyramid, did not please everyone. The building was initially not equipped with any form of air-conditioning and the interior became very hot during the day and cold at night. Fans stirred the air, but did little to help. Air-conditioning has now been installed, but the location of the building is far from ideal and it will always be difficult to maintain the controlled atmosphere which the boat needs. The fluctuations in temperature and humidity suffered by the boat before its environment was stabilised have caused some of the timbers to shrink and crack. The boat is now approximately one metre shorter than when it was first restored.

There have been many plans for the Giza Necropolis as a whole and gradually these are becoming a reality. One idea proposed is to excavate an underground cavern, near the

Pyramids, which will be large enough to take the first boat and provide far more stable conditions. This new museum would be large enough to include the second ship too and plans are being formulated for a preliminary excavation and study of the timbers of the second pit. Now that the archaeologists are aware that the contents of the pit are far from stable, excavation is essential if we are to learn anything about this second ship before the timbers decay completely. Once excavation is complete, although the timbers may not survive, we will, at worst, have gained much information. At best, we may well have another completely restored and reconstructed boat.

An interesting point is that many of the other, now empty, boat pits around the Great Pyramid and at other sites, such as Sakkara, are actually boat-shaped, with curved sides. Perhaps these contained smaller vessels and it was only the largest which needed to be dismantled and neatly placed in rectangular pits. One of the Giza pits has a long sloping ramp leading from ground-level to the main pit, down which perhaps a complete vessel was dragged.

30. Fifth Dynasty sailing boat with a single mast and hedgehog decoration at the bow

Some of the boat pits adjacent to the Great Pyramid may, however, never have actually contained real boats. They are boat-shaped and may have been stone "boats" connected with the solar and stellar cults rather than actual vessels.

This can be better seen in the boat pits of the Second Pyramid at Giza. Five pits have been discovered associated with this pyramid, built for Khafra. Four are unusual in that, from the surface, each appears to be a long narrow trench cut in the rock. The bottom of each pit, however, opens out, undercuts the rectangular trench and is carved to represent the interior of a boat. The solid rock is even carved to indicate the planks of the boat. Two of these "boats" are complete with cabins.

Two of the pits were roofed over and are believed to represent the boats needed for the deceased King at night, the stellar boats. The other two pits appear to have been left open and represent the day boats, the solar boats of the King.

No trace of any real wooden boats has been found in these pits and the undercut features and details of planking carved from the rock indicate that they were intended to be stone boats. If a stone statue could become, in the minds of the ancient Egyptians, a replacement body, then a stone boat would be as acceptable as a wood boat, with the additional benefit of being far more durable.

Perhaps Khufu was the last of the Old Kingdom kings to bury a full sized boat, as the boat pits at the later Old Kingdom pyramids at Abusir, Abu Rouash and Sakkara have revealed no evidence that they once contained real vessels.

That the majority of the boat pits, large and small, when excavated were found to be empty is no real surprise now that we know the size of some of the vessels they may have once contained and the mass of timber involved. Wood was a rare and valuable commodity and could easily be re-used in other boats, or be cut up to make items of furniture and coffins. Very little of the wood would have been wasted, with even the fragments used for ushabti figures or smaller furniture elements. Robbing the boat-pits would have been much easier and cheaper than an expedition to the Lebanon for new timber. We do not know when most of these pits were emptied, but with the timber being preserved so well in the dry climate, it would still be usable hundreds, if not thousands, of years after its first use.

For evidence of other Old Kingdom vessels, we have to refer to the many reliefs which have survived. Most of the boats shown in

31. Sixth Dynasty boat

connection with the kings or in religious scenes appear to be similar in appearance to the boat of Khufu. Working vessels are shown with a hedgehog head decorating the bow of the vessel.

The working boats have cabins similar to the royal boats and forked supports at either end of the cabin, which were used to support the mast when it was lowered. The foot of the mast (bipod or single) fitted against stout timbers, known as "knees", fixed to the cross beams and deck of the boat. The mast was not fixed permanently into place and could be raised when the use of the sail was required and lowered when the boat was propelled by oars. Once hauled upright, the mast was secured in place by rope stays running from the mast top to the hull of the boat, and the foot of the mast was lashed to the knees.

Steering of these vessels was by means of oars and some are shown with three steering oars, instead of the usual one or two.

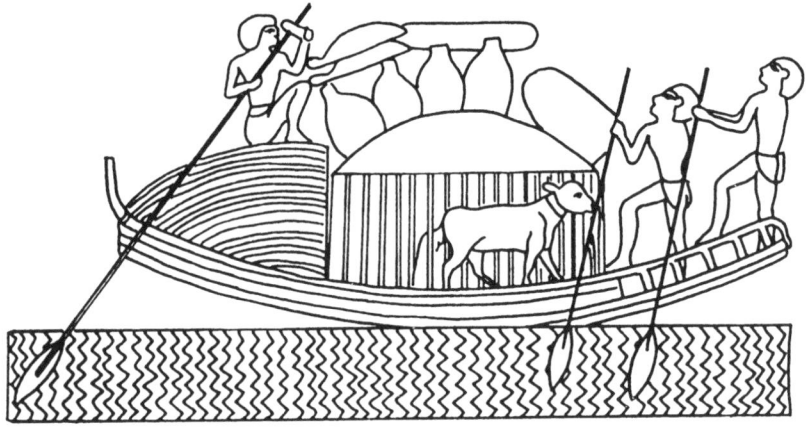

32. Old Kingdom cargo boat

In the Fourth and Fifth Dynasties, the sails are shown as being narrower at the base than the top. It would appear that the sails, made of heavy linen, were composed of bolts of material joined horizontally, rather than vertically.

By the Sixth Dynasty, the working boats appear to be built with flat bottoms, which gave them far more space below decks for cargo and also made them easier to construct.

These vessels have blunt bows and sterns. Cabins are shown as being brightly decorated; either they were painted, or the scenes represent coloured woven mats. Many tomb scenes survive which show small loaded cargo boats propelled by oars and larger vessels under sail.

The Dahshur Boats

During the season of 1894–1895, Jacques de Morgan was excavating at Dahshur, about thirty-three kilometres south of Cairo. Concentrating on the remains of a mud brick pyramid and subsidiary buildings, he identified the site as the burial place of King Senuseret III of the Twelfth Dynasty (around 1841 B.C.).

Having completely excavated the interior of the complex (and finding some spectacular jewellery belonging to the daughters and wives of the King) de Morgan moved outside the enclosure walls in an attempt to find the original subterranean entrance to the pyramid.

He discovered three wooden boat burials together, then another three, along with a wooden sledge which had been used to drag the boats across the desert from the water. Although the original account of the excavation states that six boats were found, the subsequent plans published of the excavation show either three or five.

The boats have been associated with King Senuseret III because of their discovery in part of his funerary complex, although they could equally well belong to one of the other Middle Kingdom Kings who were also buried in the same area, or to members of the royal family. The assumption is that these boats were part of the funerary equipment of the King, or that, at least, they had been used to carry funerary equipment across the river.

The boats had been buried in simple pits dug into the sand. Mud bricks had been placed beneath and around them to

33. One of the Dahshur boats being excavated in the 1894-95 season

support the bottoms and sides of the vessels. The steering oars were laid on the decks and each pit was covered with sand.

When discovered, the boats were unique examples of vessels surviving from Ancient Egypt. They attracted a great deal of interest, especially from museums in the U.S.A., which were keen to enlarge their Egyptian collections and were able to finance the purchase of such unique and spectacular items.

Two of the boats were sent to the United States. One now resides in the Carnegie Museum of Natural History in Pittsburgh; the second is in the Field Museum of Natural History in Chicago. The Chicago boat has excellent documentation, which means that we can be certain that it came from the Dahshur excavation. The Carnegie records are scanty and the certain proof that the boat also came from Dahshur is missing. Comparison of these boats, however, has left little doubt that they are both of the same date, size and method of construction and must have come from the same site. Two other boats from the same site remained in Egypt and are now in the Cairo Museum. The whereabouts of the fifth recorded boat is unknown. Such a large and important object would be known, if it had been sent out of Egypt to a foreign museum, and it is presumed that it was never removed from the site and was re-buried.

The construction of these boats has led many experts to

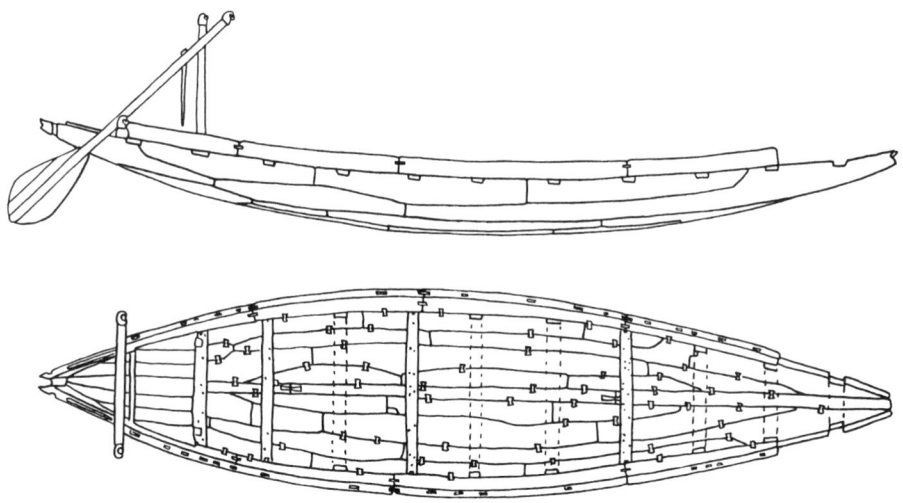

34. Plan and elevation of a Middle Kingdom boat from Dahshur in the Cairo Museum

believe that they were not necessarily functional boats. They may have been capable of making one brief journey, but they were constructed specifically to fulfil some funerary function. If this were the case, it is likely that the reuse of the boats would be forbidden and that they would be disposed of in a manner which would allow the deceased to use them in the afterlife.

The hulls of the four surviving boats are all about ten metres in length and have the same profile, with a broad cross-section, shallow body and narrow tapered ends. The bows and sterns of the boats have slots which were for the attachment of decorative stem and stern posts, now missing from all the boats.

As in the boat of Khufu, there is no conventional keel and the boat is built around a central strake. Unlike the boat of Khufu, the planks of the hull of the Dahshur boats are not held together

35. One of the two Dahshur boats, as displayed in the Cairo Museum

36. The Middle Kingdom boat from Dahshur in the Carnegie Museum

by rope. Relatively short planks of cedar have been used and the planking on either side of the vessels is symmetrical. Both sides of the hull would have been built up simultaneously to prevent undue strain on the structure.

The builders carefully matched and fitted each plank to its neighbour. The position of the mortise and tenon joints was first marked with black paint, before they were cut. In addition to the mortise and tenons, the edges of the planks are also joined together with dovetail fastenings. The dovetails are an unusual feature and may not have been very practical in a working boat, for any flexing of the timbers would cause the dovetails to pop out of their sockets. This is taken as evidence that the boats were not intended for extended use.

Some of the planks of the two Cairo boats appear to have been used before and a number of holes from the former construction have been filled with wood or plaster. This shows how precious a commodity the wood actually was and may again show that the boats were not intended for actual use on the river.

The gunwales of the boats were secured with mortise and tenon joints and also lashed with rope.

Once the hull had been assembled, beams were laid across it and fitted into slots cut in the uppermost strake. These were both pegged and lashed into place. The decks were then fitted at right-angles to the beams; in the first Cairo boat (CG4925) the deck planks are pegged to the top of the beams, whilst in the second (CG4926) they are slotted between the beams, which have a rebate cut to receive them, allowing the deck planks to be removed easily if necessary.

Traces of paint, which was laid over a thin layer of plaster, survive on the hull. The gunwales were decorated with a thin blue or black line and two thicker red stripes. Evidence from the Cairo boats indicates that the hulls were once painted green.

The steering oars remain, together with elements of the stanchions which supported them. The oars were once equipped with decorative finials, but these have not survived on either the Carnegie or Chicago boats. The Cairo examples are equipped with blue painted falcon heads.

The blades of the oars were originally painted with a pattern of lotus flowers and Udjat eyes and the stanchions with coloured bands. The paint was clearly visible when the boats were first excavated, but has since faded and is not visible on the boats today, although remains of the layer of plaster beneath the paint

37. Detail of a hawk's head decorating one of the Dahshur boats in the Cairo Museum

still survives.

The Carnegie boat is the only one of the four surviving to have been extensively studied. It was dismantled in 1975, recorded and finally reassembled in 1989. The Cairo boats are described in the Cairo Museum Catalogue *Models of Ships and Boats*, published in 1913. (Although not models, being unique items they did not warrant a catalogue on their own and were added to this volume). Both the Cairo boats are on display today in the Egyptian Museum.

A few other finds have been made which are contemporary with the Dahshur boats. At Lisht, another Twelfth Dynasty site, many sturdy timbers of acacia and tamarisk were found close to the Pyramid of Senuseret I. These planks are some ten centimetres in thickness and were joined with mortise and tenon joints and also lashed together. The timbers probably came from

38. Reconstruction of the Middle Kingdom boat from Dahshur in the Carnegie Museum

a working boat, but they had deliberately been cut apart for re-use. Recent excavations have uncovered the remains of a mile-long road, with timbers buried along its entire length. This is probably the road built when the pyramid of the King was being constructed, along which the building blocks would have been dragged to the site.

A model boat from the same period also survives. Found in the mastaba of one Imhotep, it is 1.95 metres in length and is the only recorded model which has an individually planked hull. A similar number of planks to the Dahshur boats are used in the construction and the proportions are similar, with a length of five times the width. This model is painted green with red and blue stripes along the gunwale.

With the surviving examples of the boat of Khufu and the Dahshur boats, we have evidence of how the larger and smaller vessels were made. The skills of the boat builders in constructing a hull from smaller pieces of timber can clearly be seen and these techniques were used for the remainder of Egyptian boatbuilding history.

Herodotus described Egyptian boatbuilding when he visited Egypt in the fifth century B.C., and he could well be describing one of the Dahshur boats .... *"from the acacia tree they cut planks three feet long, which they put together like courses of brick, building up the hull as follows; they join these three foot lengths together with long, close-set dowels; when they have built up a hull in this fashion they stretch crossbeams over them. They use no ribs and they caulk seams from the inside using papyrus fibres"*. Techniques of boat building obviously changed very little down the centuries. One Twentieth Dynasty tomb painting clearly shows a small fishing boat built of relatively small timbers and exactly "like courses of bricks" as described by Herodotus.

It would have been the wooden boats which undertook the long sea journeys, for there is no real evidence of papyrus boats undertaking such voyages. Thor Heyerdal proved that they were capable of sea travel and it could be argued that it must have been papyrus vessels which sailed to Lebanon to bring back the cedar timbers used for the first large wooden ships. Exactly how much cargo a papyrus vessel could carry, stacked on its deck, must remain a matter of conjecture but the bulk of cargoes which headed to and from Egypt would have been carried on wooden boats. Small wooden boats would have carried larger timbers, which could be used to build bigger boats, which could then be used to carry still larger timbers.

Construction of most wooden vessels throughout the Dynastic Period was similar to the construction of Khufu's boat, with the hulls being held together with rope. From the New Kingdom the larger vessels were built with a more conventional keel, rather than just a centre plank. This gave the hull much greater strength, which was essential for those vessels which were to sail in the open sea, even more so if they were to carry large and heavy cargoes. To give additional strength, the hulls of larger

54

39. Wooden fishing boat from the tomb of Ipy, Twentieth Dynasty

vessels from the end of the Old Kingdom onwards were equipped with thick ropes running around the hull, just below deck level. These rope strengtheners are known as "truss-girdles". Yet more rigidity was provided by a "hogging-truss", a thick rope which ran above the deck, from the bow to the stern. The hogging-trusses could be tightened as necessary and helped to prevent the bows and sterns of the ships from sagging.

In the drawing of the relief from the temple of Sahure, both the hogging-truss and the truss-girdles can clearly be seen. On this boat, the bipod mast has been lowered and the vessel is being propelled by oars.

Nile craft had little or no need of anchors as they could always be moored to the river bank each evening. A standard piece of equipment was a long wooden stake, to which the vessels could be tied, which was hammered into the mud banks of the river. The boat of Khufu was found with such a stake and even the

40. Relief from the temple of Sahure showing a large sailing boat, with mast lowered

41. Modern model of the boat of Sahure

model boats found in the tombs are provided with this essential piece of equipment.

Boats which went to sea used simple stone anchors. Any large stone was suitable and could be secured by ropes tied around the stone, or passed through a hole bored in the stone. If boats did use anchors, it is likely to have been only in shallow water. Many anchors survive, although dating them is always difficult and most are probably Roman.

Being of shallow draft and almost flat-bottomed, boats, especially those under sail, would have needed some form of ballast to prevent them from capsizing. It is possible that in some instances the cargo served also as ballast, although in many painted scenes and reliefs, the cargo is shown on the deck. It may well be that this is an artistic convention and may not be evidence that cargo was carried this way. In the larger vessels, some space would have been available below decks, but as this area is likely to have been damp because of the unavoidable seepage of water into the hull, it would have been unsuitable for most cargoes. If ballast was needed, there has never been any shortage of suitable stone in Egypt.

Most vessels could be poled, paddled, rowed or sailed, to enable them to travel both up and downstream.

Vessels could be propelled with a pole long enough to reach the river bottom, although probably only the smallest used this method of propulsion and then only in the shallowest water. Paddling is shown in a relief from the funerary temple of King Userkaf of the Old Kingdom. This involved the crew member raising the oar over his head and then leaning over the side of the vessel to reach the water. Each man dipped his oar into the water after the man in front in a wave-like motion. The majority of scenes and models show boats being rowed, when all the oars are used together and all the oarsmen keep the same stroke. The oarsmen sit on low stools and the oars are secured to the gunwales of the boat by rope "rowlocks".

The masts were designed to be lowered to the deck when not in use. Reliefs show single masts, but the bipod masts continued to be used extensively until the Middle Kingdom, after which single masts became the norm. The rigging of the vessels did not include rope ladders and the horizontal spacers of the bipod masts provided a ready made ladder for the crew to use when they were setting sail.

The sails themselves were made of heavy linen, or sometimes matting and were large enough to catch even the lightest of breeze on the river. To furl the sails, the top yard was lowered to rest directly above the bottom boom and the sail secured. Both the yard and the lower boom were supported by rope "lifts".

From the Middle Kingdom onwards, many models of vessels survive, in addition to the numerous representations in reliefs.

Many boats are non-papyriform in design, but were, none-theless, still constructed in a similar way to the royal boat of Khufu. Although the working vessels were wider in the beam to increase their cargo-carrying capacity, they still have elegant lines. The numerous models, which can now be found in virtually every museum with even a small Egyptian collection, show boats being rowed and under sail, boats for fishing and for pleasure

42. Model boat with oars. Twelfth Dynasty

43. Model boat from Meir, with a sail

and boats used to carry the dead on their final journey across the river Nile. Most of these models have complete crews who man the oars or trim the sails.

The models of working boats are shown with blunt bows and sterns. The full-sized examples were of wood rather than papyrus. The model of the boat used to carry the dead, complete with the mummy lying under a canopy and with attendant mourners, also represents a wooden boat, but it has the distinctive papyriform shape with the high bow and stern posts, imitating the tied bundles of papyrus, which are seen on the earlier boat of Khufu. The papyrus shape was retained for religious and funerary use.

These vessels would have sat low in the water, with the level of the river only inches from the sides (the gunwales). Seagoing vessels needed higher sides to prevent them from being swamped in heavy seas. Many Nile vessels today still sit very low in the water, especially when fully loaded and look as if they would be easily swamped in the wake of a passing tourist cruise ship. The surface of the river is usually fairly calm and it must be supposed that the ancient vessels would not be used if the surface of the water was at all rough. If an unexpected squall did hit the river, it would be the work of only a few minutes to steer the vessel to the river bank, where it could moor until conditions improved.

Some taking up of water would have been inevitable, either through leakage from the hull, or occasionally from water

44. Model boat for the dead, Middle Kingdom.

coming over the sides of the vessel, which would happen if the boat was under sail and heeled unexpectedly in a gust of wind. The time-honoured method of baling out the vessel would be used, using clay pots as balers. We have no evidence of any wrecks of ancient Egyptian vessels, but the odd accident must have occurred on the river as well as losses at sea. However good the sailors were, the occasional disaster must have been inevitable.

On several of the models from the tomb of Meketra, a man is shown standing at the bows holding a length of rope, from which hangs a cylindrical object. This may represent a fender, but fenders are more usually used to protect the sides of vessels, not the bow. It is likely that this object is a weight and line, used to test the depth of the water. Even in waters well known to the sailors, the underwater mud-banks could present a real problem to navigation. No boatmaster would wish to suffer the indignity

45. Decorated steering oar from a model boat of the Middle Kingdom

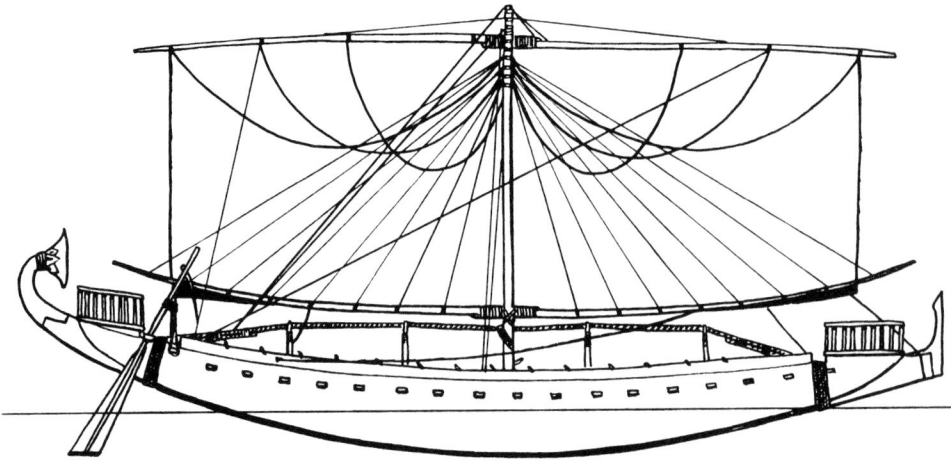

46. Drawing of a boat from Queen Hatshepsut's expedition to Punt

of grounding his vessel close to the riverbank, especially as refloating it would be a far from easy task.

We know that the ancient boats were capable of carrying huge cargoes. Queen Hatshepsut of the Eighteenth Dynasty organised a large trading expedition to the land of Punt (which is generally thought to be part of modern Somalia). The story of this voyage is told on the walls of her funerary temple at Deir el Bahri. Detailed scenes show the vessels used and the cargoes they carried.

The illustration here shows a reconstruction of one of the Punt vessels, based on the reliefs. This type of boat is seen in the later Dynasties and can almost be considered a "classic" Egyptian boat.

Probably built of cedar, the boat is around twenty-five metres long, with room on either side for fifteen oarsmen. The shape of the hull is semi-papyriform and the stern post of the vessel ends in a large, decorative papyrus flower. A small platform is provided at the bow and the stern, but there is no central cabin. Like the earlier boat of Sahure, a large, thick hogging-truss runs the length of the hull to both strengthen it and keep its shape. The ends of the large deck beams can be seen projecting through the hull above the water level.

The cargo would have been stored both on and below the deck. The large sail is supported by both upper and lower yard arms. The lower yard has each end raised by rope "lifts", which would prevent the yard and sail from dipping into the water if the boat should heel over in the wind. These large sails were originally developed to catch the wind coming directly from behind the vessel, which was the prevailing situation in Egypt. The sailing vessels would have found it more difficult to cope with the wind coming from any other direction and when this was the case, the oars would be the safest option.

One amazing fact about this expedition to Punt is that the vessels had to reach the Red Sea from the river Nile. There was no link between river or the Mediterranean and the Red Sea, so the only way the vessels could physically get there was overland across the desert, through Wadi Hammamat to Quseir on the Red Sea coast. The unique method of construction, with rope holding the vessels together, meant that they could be dismantled, physically carried across the desert and reassembled there. After the completion of the journey, the vessels would have been dismantled and they and their cargoes would have been manhandled back to Coptos and then reassembled and sailed to Thebes. Queen Hatshepsut obviously considered the journey to Punt so important and historic an event that she had a record of it made in her temple. The fine reliefs show the boats loaded with the exotic produce of Punt, which included live trees in pots, destined for the temple and palace gardens.

It is possible that some of the vessels could have been pulled across the desert in one piece. The hull would have been capable of withstanding this, and with sufficient manpower the idea is not as far-fetched as it may seem. Whatever way the vessels were transported, it was a remarkable achievement and we have no records of any other such large-scale expedition. Once the trade

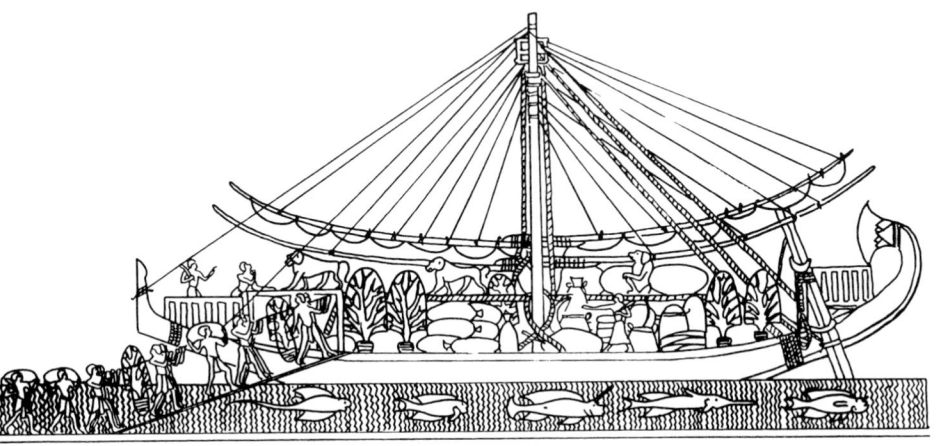

47. New Kingdom boat loaded with cargo. From the temple of Queen Hatshepsut

48. Modern model of a boat from Queen Hatshepsut's expedition to Punt

link had been established, it may have been possible to maintain communications with Punt by land and by using native Red Sea vessels, which removed the major task of transporting Egyptian boats. It is also possible that the Punt boats went on a one-way journey, in that they were left on the Red Sea coast for future use there. Bringing them back, valuable though they were, may have been considered an unnecessary extravagance, especially if they could continue to be used for trade in the Red Sea.

It is also from the reign of Queen Hatshepsut that we have records of the building of some of the largest wooden vessels in Ancient Egypt, or indeed in the ancient or modern world. Huge barges were built to transport her two obelisks from Aswan, where they had been quarried, to Thebes, where they were set up in the temple of Amun at Karnak.

The surviving, standing obelisk of Queen Hatshepsut at Karnak is 29.6 metres high and, with an estimated weight of 323 tons, is amongst the largest obelisks ever erected.

Obelisks were usually set up in pairs before the temple

entrances. Hatshepsut's successor, Thutmose III, set up many obelisks, one, of which is now in Rome and measures 32.18 metres. The famous unfinished obelisk at Aswan, which cannot be dated to any specific reign, and which was completed on three sides, but never cut free from the rock, is 41.75 metres in length. At the base, it is a staggering 4.2. metres wide on each side and its total weight, had it been completed, is estimated at 1,168 tons, which would have made it heavier than any other piece of stone ever handled by the Ancient Egyptians. It would have needed a correspondingly enormous vessel to transport it north to its planned resting place.

It is estimated that the obelisk barges may have been over ninety-five metres in length, thirty-two metres wide and have had a displacement of an amazing 7,300 tonnes when loaded. Too large to be equipped with a sail and not very manoeuverable, these barges would have been towed downstream by smaller vessels, taking full advantage of the current to travel from Aswan

49. The surviving standing obelisk of Queen Hatshepsut in the temple of Amun at Karnak

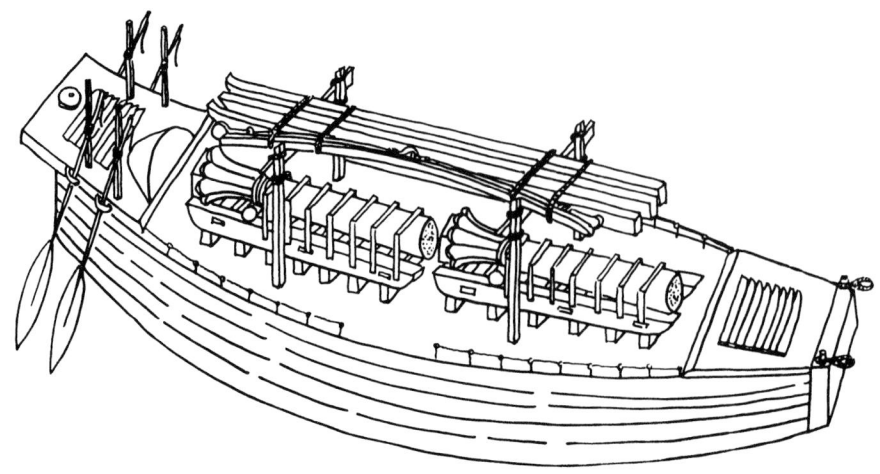

50. *Reconstruction of a barge to carry large columns in the Old Kingdom*

to Thebes. The current would have provided most of the motive power, with the smaller craft providing some degree of steerage.

Hatshepsut's reliefs showing these barges are very detailed, but it is still unclear if they were built to carry one or two obelisks. The barge could have been taken back for a second journey, but Björn Landström, author of *Ships of the Pharaohs*, considers that it would have been almost impossible to have towed a vessel of this size upstream against the current of the river. The only option would have been to dismantle the barge, transport all the pieces in separate vessels and then reassemble the barge at Aswan, in itself a mammoth undertaking.

Hatshepsut was by no means the first, or the last to erect huge obelisks, or colossal statues of granite, so this type of craft must have been a fairly regular sight on the river from the time of the Old Kingdom onwards. Reliefs from the causeway of Unas at Sakkara show a large vessel carrying granite columns.

Some of these columns remain *in situ* at the site of his Valley Temple and one is now in the British Museum. Clearly it would have been possible to re-use such a barge, the life-span of which could well have exceeded the reign of one particular monarch, but it is not difficult to imagine the vast effort in terms of manpower, materials and time needed to move the monumental blocks which are still admired today in the Egyptian temples.

If, as suggested, these barges were dismantled, their long use over many years is quite likely, for any damaged or worn component parts could easily be replaced. Perhaps Hatshepsut's barges were not new. Thutmose I, who ruled before Hatshepsut, would have needed such vessels to transport his obelisks to Karnak, as would her immediate successor Thutmose III who also erected obelisks at the main temples. If the working life of such barges were extended this way, then perhaps even Ramesses II was able to use the same vessels for the transportation of his obelisks to the temple of Luxor.

There are more obelisks today outside Egypt than remaining in the country. At least three (Paris, London and New York) were only moved in the last century, and the difficulties encountered in shipping them taxed even the minds of the nineteenth century engineers and shipbuilders.

The illustration shows a reconstruction of an obelisk barge, with two obelisks (weighing well over two thousand tons) secured on deck. This restoration is based upon scenes carved on temple walls whose exact interpretation is difficult. In the reliefs, the obelisks are shown end to end on the deck of the barge, but this is assumed to be an artistic convention, which demanded that both obelisks be clearly seen. In the reconstruction, the obelisks have been placed, as is more likely, side by side.

To provide extra strength, the vessel was built with several decks and the ends of the deck beams can be seen protruding through the hull. Several large hogging trusses run from the bow to the stern to prevent them from collapsing under the tremendous weight of the obelisks loaded on the main deck.

Loading the obelisks on to the barge would also have been a difficult task and one which necessitated great care to ensure that the obelisks were not subjected to stresses which might fracture the stone. It was also vital that the boats were loaded evenly, in

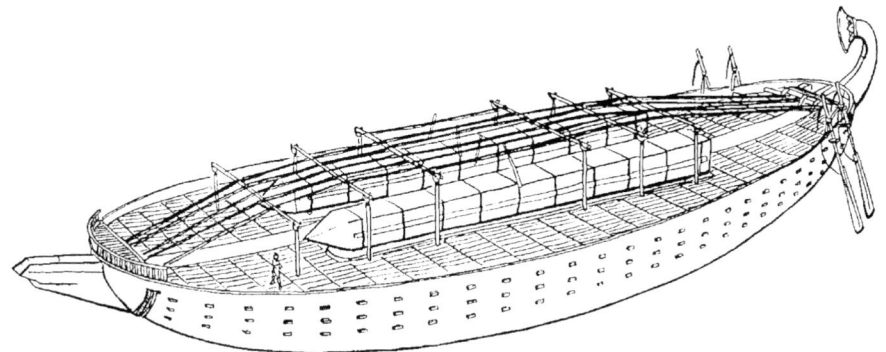

51. Reconstruction of the obelisk barge of Queen Hatshepsut

52. *Model boats as found in the Treasury of the tomb of Tutankhamun*

such a way as to avoid damaging the hull or even capsizing the vessel. It is presumed that the obelisks were moved over a specially dug canal, where they were supported on timbers, and that the barge was moved beneath them. At the time of the inundation, the water level would rise until the floating barge lifted the obelisks. A very large canal would be needed and a similar one required at the point of disembarkation, but these have not been found and this method must remain conjectural. One other idea is that the barges were secured close to the river bank and that a mud embankment was raised around and over them. The obelisks would then be manhandled into place over the barge, when the embankment would be removed. Whatever method was used, the effort required in building the barges, cutting the obelisks, moving and erecting them was enormous.

Tutankhamun's tomb contained examples of many model boats, both working boats and ritual models needed by the King in the afterlife.

Thirty-five model boats were found in the Annex and Treasury of the small tomb in the Valley of the Kings. The models show

53. Modern model of a boat, based upon ancient models from the tomb of Tutankhamun

many types of boat from large wooden sailing boats to small papyrus rafts. Unlike earlier models, Tutankhamun's model fleet was not provided with model crew members.

Whilst these models are sometimes very detailed, especially the rigging, the shapes of the hulls have been distorted by the model makers. A model made by the Science Museum in London corrects the shape of the hull to what would be expected in a full-sized boat. The models have painted designs at both bow and stern, which cover a large area of the hull. In reality, with the hulls floating low in the water, the area available for decoration would have been much smaller. With painted hulls and cabins, and even coloured sails, these vessels would have presented a magnificent sight on the river.

Some of the models have no sails and no oars (apart from the usual steering oars at the stern) which indicates that they were intended to be towed. The towing of vessels was probably a common occurrence, as it is still on the river today.

Papyriform craft are shown with decorated bows and sterns. The exact use of some of these boats is not certain but they are probably connected with the requirements of the King in the afterlife. Some boats are clearly designed for just one passenger as they are provided with a decorated throne amidships.

On one model (*Fig 55*) the papyrus bow and stern are identical to those of the boat of Khufu, who pre-dates Tutankhamun by over one thousand years. This boat was probably intended to carry the dead King across the heavens when he joined his fellow Gods in the afterlife.

The earthly vessels made for the Gods would have presented an even more splendid sight, for they were papyriform in shape and covered in gold. The bow and stern was decorated with the image of the God and a shrine on the deck housed the sacred image. These sacred barges, when used, were towed in great processions on the river.

The sacred bark of Amun is depicted on a pink quartzite block from the Red Chapel of Queen Hatshepsut at Karnak, which was either never completed, or demolished by later builders. The decorated blocks were discovered used as filling material in a later Pylon.

One block shows the sacred Bark, which bears an effigy of a Ram, an animal sacred to Amun, at the bow and stern. A shrine amidships is decorated with "Djed" and "Sa" symbols. (Similar decorations in blue covered the outer, gold-covered shrine which protected the body of Tutankhamun in his tomb). The shrine, which would have contained the image of the God, is surmounted by a lighter canopy which is supported by poles identical to those found on the much earlier boat of Khufu.

The boat is steered by Thutmose III, and the figure of Hatshepsut (shown here as a king) stands before the shrine.

A large sculpture in black granite, now in the British Museum, was made for Queen Mutemuia, wife of Thutmose IV. The figure of the Queen, which is now missing, originally sat on a throne on a boat, with the figure of a divine vulture (Mut) standing behind her. The bow of this vessel is decorated with the head of the goddess Hathor, and forms a rebus on the Queen's name: Mutemuia means "Mut in the Boat"!

Other sacred vessels are portrayed in tombs and a good example can be seen on the green breccia sarcophagus of Nectanebo II of the Thirtieth Dynasty, in the British Museum. These representations show much lighter and more delicate vessels, which clearly are papyriform in shape. These boats were for the use of the Gods to cross the Heavens and represent the

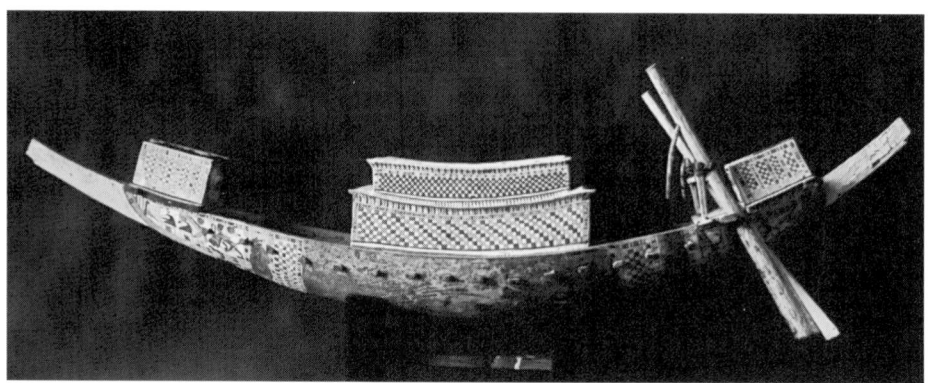

54, 55 & 56. Model boats from the tomb of Tutankhamun

idea of a vessel, rather than representing a practical sailing craft. With boats playing such an important part in the lives of the Ancient Egyptians, it is no real surprise that it was imagined that the Gods used boats for their travels. The sun and moon were imagined as sailing across the sky in celestial boats.

We know that Egyptian wooden boats must have sailed on the open sea, trading with the countries around the eastern

57. Decorated block from the Red Chapel of Queen Hatshepsut at Karnak, showing the sacred bark of the god Amun

Mediterranean. Hard evidence of boats designed for this purpose is rare, but in the reign of Ramesses III (1182–1151 B.C.) at least one naval battle was fought in the open sea. The scenes were carved on the walls of Ramesses's funerary temple at Medinet Habu. Constructed along traditional lines, these boats nevertheless show several new developments worth noting.

The bows of the boat appear to be made into a "ram" – a re-enforced bow which could be used to sink other boats. The vessels would be sailed or rowed directly at the enemy and the ram used to puncture the hull of the opposing vessel. There is, however, some doubt as to whether the boats were actually used in this way, for on the assumption that they were still built essentially the same way as earlier vessels, with a shell

58. Black granite sacred boat of Queen Mutemuia, wife of Thutmose IV

construction, laced together, they are unlikely to have been strong enough to have survived the shock of the impact if used to ram other vessels.

A small platform was built at the top of the mast for the use of lookouts and also for archers. The additional height enabled arrows to be fired down into the crew on the decks of the enemy ships. This is the first recorded example of a "crowsnest" in the history of boats and can clearly be seen in contemporary illustrations.

The boats were fitted with high sides or gunwales, to protect the rowers from enemy attack, in particular from enemy arrows and spears. In the contemporary illustrations, the rowers are hardly visible. A raised gangway appears to run the length of the vessel to provide a fighting platform for the soldiers, whose main weapon was the bow and arrow.

The sails of boats from this period onwards are smaller and the lower yard is no longer used. To furl the sail, it was now pulled upwards to be tied to the upper yard. This has the effect of leaving the deck area clear for fighting. It is considered that this innovation may have been introduced from a neighbouring country, such as Greece.

One sail from an ancient boat survives and was found in the most unlikely of places: a mummy, dating from the first century B.C., in the Guimet Museum in Lyon. This mummy was unwrapped and scientifically examined in 1986. The large

59. Ritual boat from the sarcophagus of Nectanebo II

amount of linen and bandages covering the body was also examined. Pieces of linen which had been used as packing were recovered and these appeared to be pieces of the same object. It was realised that these pieces could be reassembled and this process was helped by reinforced bands of thicker linen which were sewn to the lighter material. These bands formed a rough grid pattern.

60. Warship of Ramesses III, scene from the temple of Medinet Habu

When the pieces were laid out in the correct order, using the reinforcing strips as a guide, the result was a sheet of linen in a trapezoid shape some 5.5 metres high and between 4.5 and 5.5 metres wide. It was recognised as a sail, especially as a piece of a wooden ring and fragments of rope still remained attached to the edges where it was once tied to the yard. It is a unique survival of such an object and is similar to representations, which are contemporary, of the sails of boats on the walls of the temple of Horus at Edfu, where the reinforcing grid pattern can also be seen.

Vessels for the remainder of Egypt's history appear to have continued to be built along the traditional lines certainly up to the time of the Ptolemaic Period (332–30 B.C) when the Greek Herodotus made his observations on the native boat-building techniques.

It is only in the last two hundred years that the river Nile has lost much of its important role as the main highway of Egypt. The advent of rail and air travel and the improved road network now mean that much movement of people and cargoes has been taken away from the river. The river still remains, however, a cheap and easy method of moving goods and even in the midst of all the new technology, the use of the river can still be the most practical way.

The building of Aswan High Dam has to some extent given the river a new lease of life, for the flow of water is constant and some of the difficulties encountered in the past at times of flood, or when the river was running low, have been removed.

The vessels constructed by the Ancient Egyptians were both practical and elegant. It is all too easy to wax lyrical about sailing ships of any period and even the dirtiest sailing vessel has an appeal to our modern eyes. The Ancient Egyptians never lost their sense of style and proportion and even the most practical of vessels, such as the obelisk barges, have fine lines and decorated bow and stern posts. This decoration serves no useful purpose and the ships would function just as well without them, but as with so many otherwise purely practical items, their makers added just that little bit extra, turning a functional object into a thing of beauty.

No other historical period before the Seventeenth Century A.D. gives us a clearer picture of its boats than does Ancient Egypt. For classical antiquity we have had, until recent times at least, to rely on ambiguous pictures and simple models. Over the last two

61. A modern working felucca, carrying stone, at Cairo

62. *Modern feluccas on the river Nile at Luxor*

decades, underwater archaeology has improved greatly and many Classical period shipwrecks have been discovered and excavated.

It is possible that other seafaring nations, such as the Phoenicians, Greeks and Romans built their boats on the same principles as the Ancient Egyptians, or at least were able to use and build on the considerable experience and expertise of the Egyptian boat-builders. Many of these ancient vessels have hulls constructed in a similar way to the earlier Egyptian vessels. How much was borrowed from the Egyptians can only be a matter of conjecture, but it would be surprising if Egyptian boats visiting foreign ports did not greatly influence the boat-building of those countries. Man has always been quick to recognise a good thing when he sees it and throughout maritime history, any new developments by one nation have always been quickly copied, and sometimes improved on, by others.

A clear evolution of sailing craft has been established from the early Middle Ages to the Nineteenth century A.D. It is recognised that the ships of the Middle Ages owe much to the ships of Classical antiquity and if we can trace the connection back to Ancient Egypt, we have an unbroken evolution of sailing craft from the earliest papyrus rafts right up to modern times.

The prospect of further exciting discoveries is always present in Egypt and somewhere there may even be the wreck of a sea-going Ancient Egyptian vessel waiting to be discovered. Any new disoveries will add to the already considerable knowledge we have of transport by water in Ancient Egypt and in the ancient world.

II TRANSPORT ON LAND

"Necessity is the mother of invention". It is a curious fact that one of the greatest civilisations in the world flourished without the use of the wheel – an invention considered by many to be one of man's greatest inventions and essential to the development of any civilisation. Why was the wheel not used in Egypt until relatively late in the country's long history? The answer is that there was simply no significant need for the use of a wheel.

The importance of the river Nile as the main highway of Egypt has already been stressed. With the river running the length of the country and the numerous irrigation canals, there would have been few temples, palaces or homes more than a hundred yards or so from a navigable stretch of water. All goods could be transported easily by water and once on land could be carried by hand or on the backs of donkeys. There was no real need for carts or wagons.

Without using the wheel, the Egyptians still managed to build some of the largest and most spectacular buildings that the world has seen. In all probability wheels would have been of little practical use, for the building blocks used were far too large and too heavy to be carried on a wooden-wheeled cart. The relative scarcity of wood in Ancient Egypt would have made the building of such carts difficult and overcoming the practical and technical difficulties of building carts to carry and move great weights would have probably proved impossible.

Wheels would have been, in any event, a far from practical method of transport on either the agricultural land or the desert where they would have quickly become bogged down in either mud or sand. The additional labour required to lay a more solid road surface would have seemed unnecessary when alternative methods of transport were available.

The Egyptians were, however, well aware of the wheel, which **was** used in a minor way. A unique representation from the Old Kingdom, found in the tomb of Kaemhesit at Sakkara, shows men climbing up a scaling ladder which is fitted with solid wheels at the base. The wheels enabled the ladder to be easily and quickly manoeuvred into place and two men are using baulks of timber to prevent the wheeled base of the ladder from moving. Some of the men carry axes, tucked into the back of their kilts, others have embedded the axe heads in the wall they are scaling and are using them as hand-holds to help their ascent.

Transport on land, at least until the introduction of the chariot,

63. A scaling ladder fitted with wheels, from the Old Kingdom tomb of Kaemhesit at Sakkara

was probably always very simple and for the majority of the population, who would have rarely made long journeys, involved travelling on foot. In ancient times, the people would walk from their homes to their place of work, which was unlikely to be far away. Travel over longer distances for most of the population would have been rare and most Egyptians lived and died in the town or village of their birth. This is not so unusual, for it is only in the last two hundred years that the populations of modern countries have had the ability to move easily over great distances.

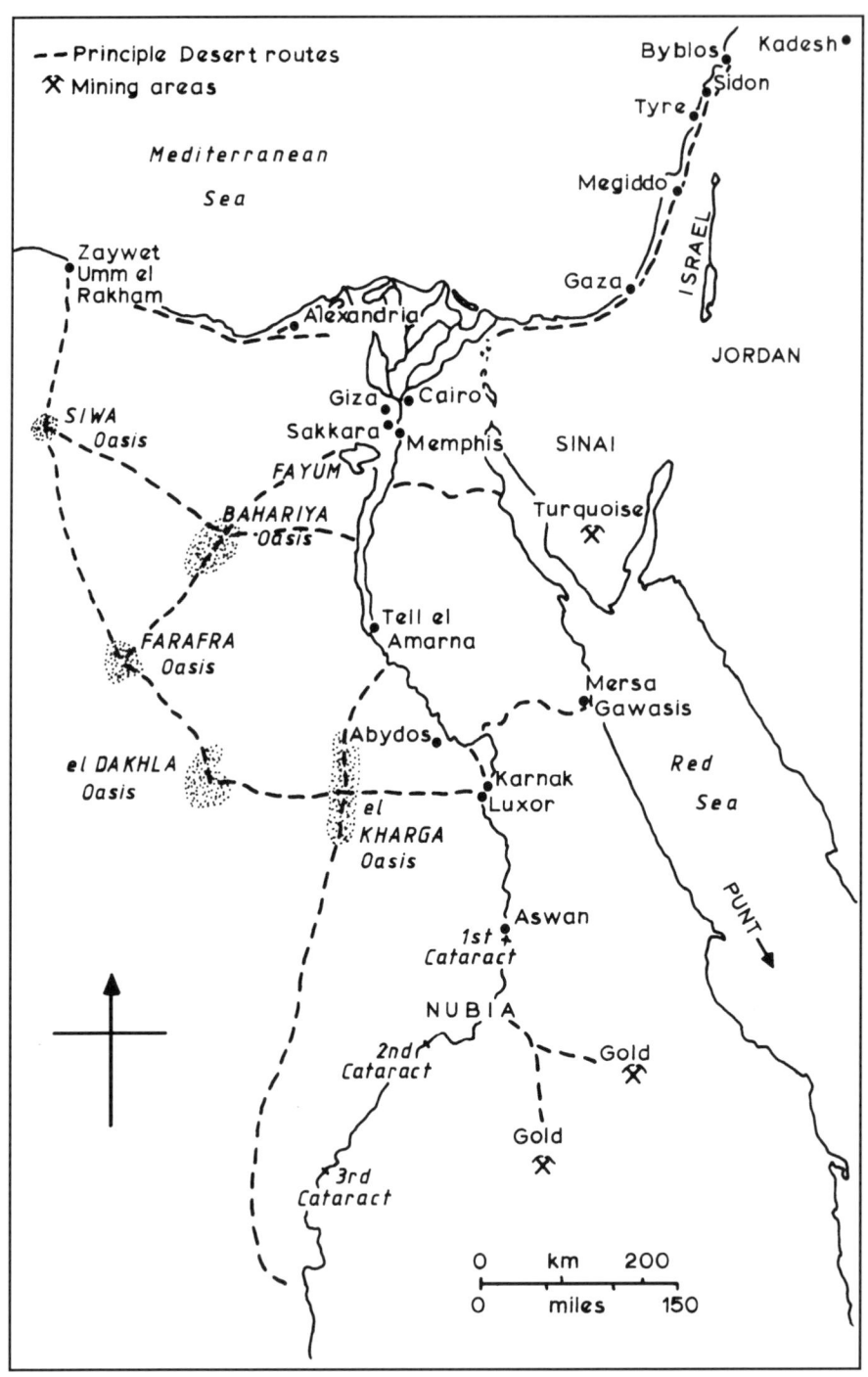

64. *Map of Egypt and the neighbouring countries, showing the principal desert routes and the road network*

(a) The Road Network

An effective road network evolved very early in Egypt's history and to some extent grew side by side with the irrigation system. When irrigation canals were dug, the soil excavated was placed on both sides of the ditch, forming embankments. The pathways and roads were made on the top of these embankments, which is still the practice in Egypt today. The mud of the embankment was soon compressed into a firm road surface by the passage of men and animals. There is a distinct advantage to be gained by having roads on an elevated embankment, for they are well clear of the water levels (except perhaps during the period of inundation, when the majority of the smaller roads would have been flooded) and visibility is excellent from them. This made them safer for travellers who could clearly see where they were going and could themselves be seen. The hieroglyph for "road" shows a road built on an embankment, with papyrus growing from the ditch below 𓂝𓃀𓎛𓈖. Most of these roads would have linked villages to the fields, temples and burial grounds.

On the edge of the river valley, the desert routes branched off from the network of canals and roads in Egypt itself. Most of these routes ran along dry, open valleys. These valleys, known as wadis, were chosen since, despite the fact that the rivers which once formed them had long since dried up, water could often be found by sinking wells along the valley floor. Water was never a problem in Egypt, but for any long journeys it was essential that good water could be found en-route, as it would not have been possible to transport sufficient water to sustain animals and humans. The surface of the ground at the bottom of the wadis is usually fairly solid, level and free of any major obstructions.

On the east bank of the river, routes led to mines in the Arabian mountains and to the Red Sea. We know that these routes were well travelled throughout Egypt's long history, for graffiti dating to all periods of Ancient Egyptian history cover the boulders along the wayside. Other routes carried gold from the mines in Nubia, turquoise from Sinai and produce from Punt and Coptos.

On the west bank of the river, desert routes led to the Kharga Oasis and to the Baharia Oasis. All the great oases were reached by these routes, which continued as far south as Nubia.

In the north-west, the route to the Mediterranean left the Delta and turned towards Libya, and in the north-east, towards Palestine. The Kings of the New Kingdom built a series of forts guarding these important routes, along which travelled the Egyptian armies which expanded the Empire and the goods and tribute from the conquered countries.

These routes were not generally paved, but the constant passage of men and animals compacted the already hard ground and clearly marked the way. Some are still visible today even though they have not been used for hundreds of years.

In Egypt itself, hard evidence for the actual ancient roads is lacking, but in many cases this is for the simple reason that they are still being used today. Many modern routes and roads still follow the lines of the ancient paths and roads.

A rare, paved, Ancient Egyptian road has recently been discovered, running from the Faiyum depression towards modern Cairo. The existence of this road had been noted before, but no one had realised its age or length before. Identified by the U.S. Geological Survey in Denver, the road runs for 11.5 kilometres and is built from flagstones and petrified wood found in the area. The road is perfectly straight and the best preserved parts are 2.1 metres wide. Artifacts found along the road show that it was in use in the Fifth and Sixth Dynasties of the Old Kingdom, between 2498 and 2181 B.C.. The road starts at the basalt deposits of Gebel Qatrani. Basalt was greatly prized and extensively used during this period for building and sculpture and the road would have been used to move the large stones, dragged on sledges, to the shores of Lake Moeris, where they could then be transported by water.

The other main surviving paved roads are relatively short in length and connect the temples of ancient Thebes. One paved road runs from the temple of Amun at Karnak to the temple of Luxor and others connect the temple of Amun with the temple of Mut. These roads are ceremonial ways and are lined for their entire length by either ram or human-headed sphinxes. They would have been used for the main processions of the Gods and by the King.

To what extent these roads may have been open to and used by the people of the city is not known.

65. The paved avenue of sphinxes leading towards the temple of Luxor

It is not certain if the roads were maintained in any way, but it must be considered more than likely that repairs were made to some of the roads and tracks, if only to fill up any potholes which had developed. This would be a relatively easy task and any new material used to fill in holes would soon be compacted into a hard surface. Such maintenance would have been essential when the roads were used for chariots, for although chariots could be, and must have been, used on rough ground, they were valuable pieces of equipment and a good, maintained road surface would do much to prolong their road-life and also ensure that they could reach a good speed.

The organisation of the Egyptian road network was so good that when the Romans, the greatest road builders of the ancient world, conquered Egypt in 30 B.C., all they needed to do was to ensure that the embankments of the canals continued to be regularly maintained and that the wells along the desert routes were kept in good repair.

There is little surviving evidence for bridges as part of the road network, although it is to be expected that some of the irrigation ditches and canals would have been bridged by simple wooden platforms, much as they are in the country today. Good quality wood is not essential for this and a bridge can be built of palm logs, which can easily bear the weight of humans and animals.

Crossing one of the larger irrigation ditches or parts of the river would entail either wading across or using a boat. Many of the irrigation ditches would not have been very deep. The main canals and the river were too large to bridge and the idea of building a bridge across such an expanse of water probably never occurred to the Ancient Egyptians. With land transport being secondary to river transport, there was no need for bridges. If goods or people had to cross the river, boats were the easiest way.

The roads away from the river valley and in the desert followed the natural contours and would go around any natural obstructions, such as deep valleys. Whilst small depressions could be filled to make a level road, the route of the road always followed the natural landscape. Where donkeys could go, man could also, so roads and pathways could be narrow and steep. It was only the use of the chariots which required the use of more level ground.

Throughout Egypt today, many of the pathways are still visible and in use. On the west bank of the river Nile at Luxor, it is possible to tread the same path used by the skilled workmen who built the Royal tombs in the Valley of the Kings. A network of paths, now used by tourists, runs over the mountains from the worker's village at Deir el Medina, to the Valley of the Kings and from the Valley to Hatshepsut's temple.

(b) Walking

Most ancient Egyptians went barefoot, as can be seen in the reliefs, paintings and sculpture.

Whilst the idea of walking without footwear is daunting to modern western man, many still go barefoot in Egypt today. Without footwear, the soles of the feet become thick and tough and even walking on the roughest of ground presents no difficulty. The warm climate of Egypt meant that footwear was not generally needed to keep the feet warm.

We do know that sandals and socks were worn and actual examples of footwear have been discovered in tombs, where they were included as part of the funerary equipment.

Made of reeds, palm leaves or leather, they are simple in design, with a single strap which passes between the first and second toes. Sandals may well have been regarded as some form of status symbol, for only the wealthy would have been able to afford to have them made, and the rich, with a more comfortable style of living, may have walked less and have actually needed the protection to their feet that the sandals offered.

Sandals protected the soles of the feet, but apart from the few leather examples which have survived and which are mostly from late in Egyptian history, the construction of most is flimsy. Many

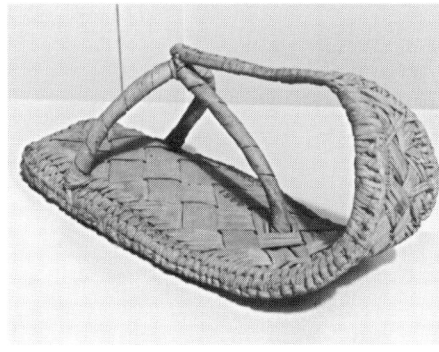

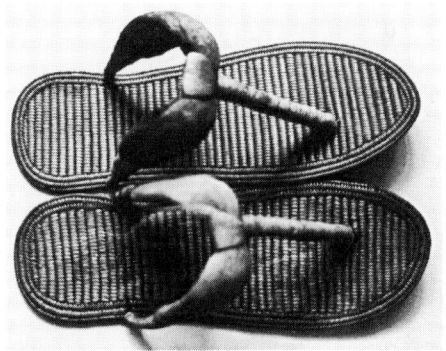

66. A sandal made of palm leaves, dating to the New Kingdom c. 1300 B.C.

67. Pair of sandals belonging to Yuya, father-in-law of King Amenhotep III

68. Model soldiers from the Middle Kingdom tomb of Mesehti at Assuit

of the examples which have survived look very clumsy and impractical, and it is likely that most of these were made specifically for the tomb, rather than having been used by the deceased in his or her lifetime.

A number of particularly fine sandals, many of which were intended for use, were found in the tombs of Yuya and Thuya and Tutankhamun, both of late Eighteenth Dynasty in date (around 1350–1330 B.C.).

Model figures have been found in a great number of tombs and most of these are barefooted. Two large models in the Cairo Museum, found in the tomb of Mesheti at Assiut and dating to the Middle Kingdom (around 2000 B.C.), depict soldiers – individuals who might be expected to travel large distances on foot. They have no footwear. One model shows Egyptian soldiers who carry spears and shields painted to imitate the hide of cattle, and the other depicts Nubian archers. Each individual figure is superbly detailed and painted and is a different height, to represent a real body of men. Both models show the soldiers with their left leg advanced, as if marching. There is often great debate amongst military historians over whether armies actually marched in step. The presumption must be that they did, for a group of individuals walking will almost naturally fall into a set and steady pace. Large groups of individuals will move faster if a steady pace is maintained and marching in step means that individuals can place themselves more closely to the rank of men in front of them.

One aid to marching for which evidence is rare is the use of a drum to keep the beat. Whilst it must be considered likely that drums were used, there are other ways to maintain a steady pace and the most obvious is singing or chanting. Workers in Egypt (and in other countries) often sang simple songs or chanted whilst working. This is especially useful where there is a repetitive action such as walking or pulling. Such chanting can still be heard in Egypt today when teams of men are working together. It is also possible that the soldiers who carried shields could keep a rhythm by beating the tough leather from which the shields were made. Making such a noise when an army is advancing both announces one's presence and can also have an intimidating effect on the enemy.

Whilst most Ancient Egyptians would have walked to their places of work, the distances involved were relatively small. The army would have travelled literally the length and breadth of the country. They would have been transported by river wherever possible, but a great proportion of their travelling would have been done on foot.

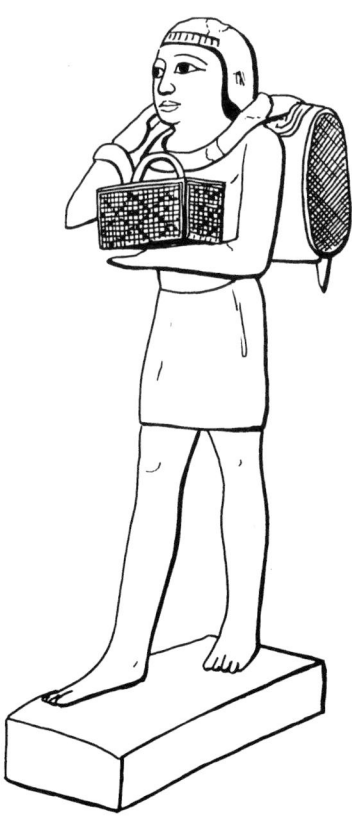

69. Old Kingdom wooden model of a porter from the tomb of Niankh-pepi at Meir

A large amount of small goods was carried, often balanced on the head, as is still seen in Egypt today. Tomb models from the Middle Kingdom survive which show servant figures, usually female, carrying large loads upon their heads, which they steady with one hand. Boxes or large baskets are shown which are often full of wine jars for the use of the deceased.

One unique Old Kingdom wooden model, dating to the reign of Pepi II (2235–2141 B.C.) represents a male porter of Niankhpepi, in whose tomb at Meir it was found. The porter carries a large basket on his back, secured by a strap around his chest and neck, almost like a modern rucksack, and holds a painted chest in front of him.

One chest found in the tomb of Tutankhamun was designed to be portable and has retractable carrying poles fixed underneath. The scale of the piece indicates that it was intended to be carried by two men.

Offering scenes from tombs show a variety of goods being carried. Some items are strung together and attached to either end of a wooden pole, which is carried across the shoulders. This yoke was often used to carry fish, which were tied together by cord passed through their gills and then secured to the ends of the yoke. Ducks and other small items were placed in baskets or nets suspended from the ends of the yoke.

Ushabti (servant figures, provided in large numbers to carry

70. *Wall painting from the New Kingdom tomb of Ramose in Western Thebes, showing the carrying of furniture to the tomb*

71. New Kingdom
tomb painting of
a man carrying
fish using a yoke

out agricultural duties for the deceased in the afterlife) are shown equipped with a yoke, which was used to carry pots of water.

Funerary scenes show all manner of household objects being carried in procession to their final resting place in the tomb. Carried by one or two men, the boxes and pieces of furniture are invariably balanced on heads.

Many larger items of furniture and funerary equipment, such as coffins and shrines, would have been carried. Whilst some of these items are provided with sledge bases, it is evident that the sledges were never actually used. Physical manhandling of the objects, or carrying by the use of wooden poles placed beneath the items, would enable large numbers of men to carry together the large and bulky objects.

As is still the case today, for unwieldy or fragile objects, there is often no alternative but to carry them on foot.

(c) Carrying Chairs

Chairs specially adapted with poles which enable them to be carried occur during many periods of history, the last examples seen in Europe being the sedan chair of the Eighteenth and Nineteenth centuries. Some of the earliest examples of this type of transport are found in Ancient Egypt.

Exactly when the carrying chair was first used is not certain. Its use enabled an individual to be carried, which marked him or her out as a person of some importance. It gave the person being carried superiority over those who were doing the carrying and over those on foot.

Chairs and stools of all types were used to indicate status in society, as can be seen in tomb reliefs from the Old Kingdom onwards. At a time when most people would sit on the floor, the use of a chair elevated those of high rank. The chairs themselves varied in height, from little more than low stools, to the full height of chairs which we use today. The higher the chair, the more important the person, with the highest of the chairs being reserved for the King himself. The elevation of the chair could be increased still further by placing it on a podium.

Unless those of high rank specifically wanted, or needed, to be on foot, the accepted method of transport befitting their status was to be carried in a chair.

In its simplest form a carrying chair is an ordinary chair to which long poles have been added to enable the chair, complete with its occupant, to be carried. All chairs would need at least two men to carry them, one at the front and one at the rear, holding the ends of the poles. Larger chairs, or those with heavier occupants, would need four men to carry them, each one taking an end of the two poles. Some reliefs survive where many more men are employed to carry one chair.

Surviving reliefs show some carrying chairs of the Old Kingdom, but one actual example has survived; the carrying chair of Queen Hetepheres, wife of King Snefru and the mother of Khufu, builder of the Great Pyramid at Giza. She died around

2580 B.C. Her original tomb was probably at Dahshur, near to her husband's Pyramids there, but her burial equipment was ultimately interred at Giza in a shaft tomb near the pyramid of Khufu. The tomb contained the sarcophagus and a canopic chest (with contents intact) along with a number of magnificent pieces of Old Kingdom furniture. For unknown reasons, the body was missing from the apparently unplundered tomb when rediscovered in 1925 by the American Egyptologist, George Andrew Reisner. What he discovered then though, was not a room full of furniture, but a room whose floor was covered in fragments of much decayed wood and plaster and pieces of the gold decoration which had once covered the furniture, all mixed together in the utmost confusion.

Reisner was faced with a daunting task, but successfully completed one of the most detailed and time consuming excavations ever seen in Egypt. By literally picking up each fragment and recording the position in which it lay in relation to all the others, he was able to discover what the objects were, how they had been placed in the tomb and, most importantly, was able to facilitate full-scale restoration of the wooden parts of the furniture to which the original decoration could be attached.

The tomb contents included a bed, two chairs (only one of which could be reconstructed) a canopy which would have

72. *The carrying chair of Queen Hetepheres as found*

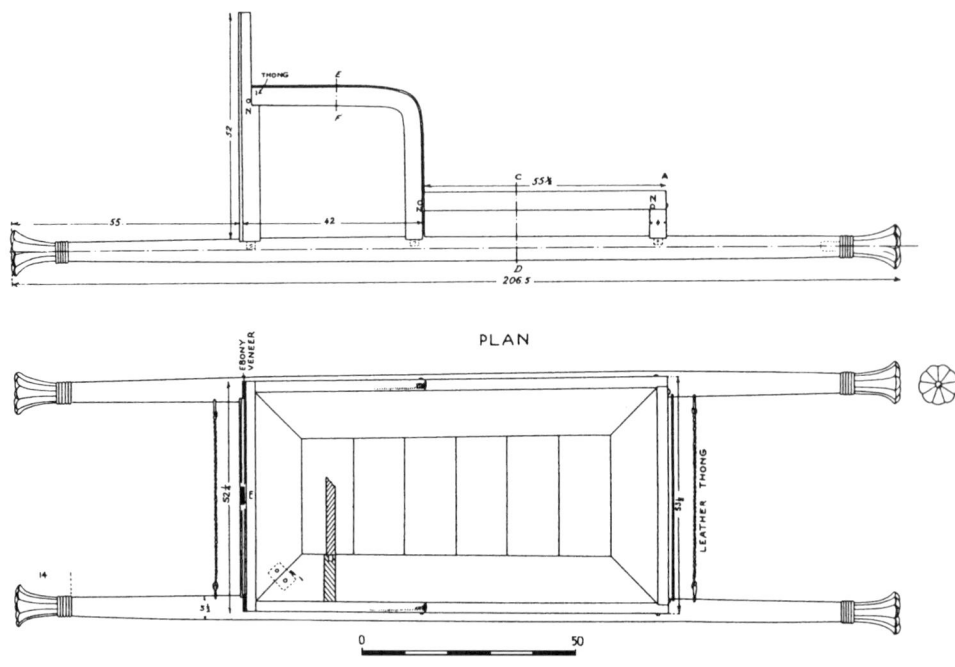

PLAN

73. Reconstructed plan and elevation of the carrying chair of Queen Hetepheres

supported curtains to cover the bed, various inlaid boxes and a carrying chair.

When discovered, the wood of the carrying chair was found to have been better preserved than some of the other wood in the tomb, but, even so, it had shrunk to about one sixth of its original volume. The heavy gold which covered parts of the chair had kept its original size and shape and restoration of these parts of the chair was relatively easy. In the photographs taken at the time of the discovery the heavy gold finials to the carrying poles can be seen as they lay on the floor of the tomb.

These gold finials had retained their original shape so well, that they were simply filled with plaster, into which slots were cut to enable the restored wooden poles to be attached.

Calculating the correct size of the undecorated timbers was not so easy and Reisner had to use the evidence of the surviving timber and the location of the various elements of the chair scattered over the floor of the tomb to determine their original position. The types of joints used in the construction were still evident and the same joints were used in the reconstruction.

The restored carrying chair, is not a conventional chair, but rather a low box supported between two poles. The box is fitted with a higher back and sides.

The width of the chair is 0.535 metres at the front and slightly narrower, 0.52 metres, at the back. All the wood in the restoration has been left plain, since it is not known if the wood was decorated in any way. It may have been painted, but no traces of any decoration survived on the original decayed woodwork.

The edges of the box, arms and back of the chair are covered in gold, incised with a reed-mat pattern. This pattern was cut into the wood before the gold overlay was applied. Ebony strips are fitted across the front of the chair back, into which have been set solid gold hieroglyphs. These hieroglyphs are superbly detailed and must rank as some of the finest ever discovered in Egypt. Similar ebony strips on the back of the chair-back give the names and titles of the Queen.

It is presumed that the Queen would have either had to sit cross-legged or have reclined in the chair. Some contemporary scenes show the occupants of similar chairs sitting on cushions, with their knees drawn up close to their chests, which does not look over-comfortable, especially for travelling longer distances. The chair of Hetepheres would have been provided with cushions, none of which appear to have been placed in the tomb. It is possible that the Queen would have sat on a low stool within the carrying chair.

74. Detail of the back of the carrying chair of Queen Hetepheres

75. *The restored carrying chair of Queen Hetepheres*

The tenon joints used in the construction of the chair were originally secured with leather thonging, which has also been used in the restoration. The knots of the thongs are hidden beneath the gold decoration.

The length of the restored poles is 2.065 metres. The original lengths of the poles of the chair could not be determined from the evidence in the tomb and Reisner made reference to contemporary illustrations in the tomb of Meresankh III, also at Giza, which showed a similar chair, from which it was possible to calculate the proportions. Two leather thongs, secured to bronze staples, are fixed between the two poles, immediately in front of and behind the box of the chair. This would provide additional strength to the chair, the joints of which must have been subject to some stress when it was in use.

Later paintings showing carrying chairs survive. In most of these, the chairs are shown with short legs, so that when rested on

76. *Carrying chair. Painted limestone relief from the tomb of Djehutihotpe. Twelfth Dynasty*

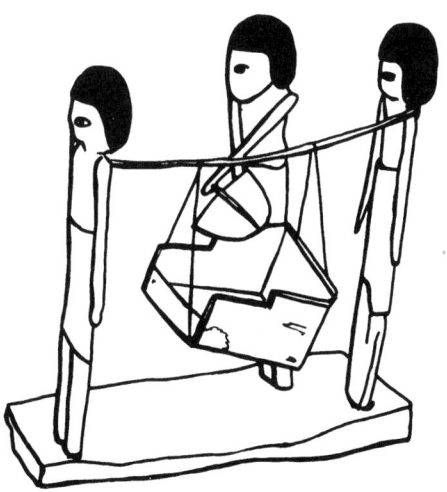

77. Middle Kingdom
tomb model of a sedan
chair

the ground the seat and, more importantly, the carrying poles, are well clear of the ground. There are no such legs on the Hetepheres chair and if rested on the ground the weight of the chair and occupant would have been borne by the elaborate decoration at the end of the poles. Either small wooden legs were fitted, but were not recognised in the debris by Reisner, or the chair would have to have been supported by a special stand whenever it was set down. As this would have involved taking the stand to the end point of any journey, this does not seem likely.

No other actual example of a carrying chair has survived.

A tomb-model of the late Eleventh or early Twelfth Dynasty, now in the Manchester Museum, appears to be a unique representation of a chair suspended from a single pole and carried by two men. It was found in the tomb of Sedment. How practical a method of transport this would have been must be open to speculation: the weight of a passenger would be a heavy load for just two men to carry in this way and the swaying of the suspended chair would have made the task still more difficult. The uniqueness of this model may indicate that the use of this type of carrying chair was limited. The model, as it is displayed today, is however, a little odd, as the carrying figures have their arms by their sides and do not support the pole on their shoulders as would be expected if the chair really was suspended from this pole. The body of the chair is similar to the body of the Hetepheres chair and it would appear that this is actually a model of a conventional carrying chair, originally supported by two poles and that it has been "restored" in this way in recent times.

The model is somewhat crude in workmanship when compared
to other contemporary models from this period. In addition to
the two men carrying the chair, a third man is shown standing by
the right side of the chair, holding a fan to cool the occupant of
the chair. Today the chair has no passenger; the figure, it
undoubtedly once contained, has been lost.

One scene survives from the New Kingdom showing the
coronation of King Horemheb, where he is shown being carried
in a chair. On this occasion he is seated on a conventional chair
or throne (similar to examples found in the tomb of
Tutankhamun). The chair appears to have been placed on a
large platform which is carried by at least twelve men at shoulder
height. It is likely that by the New Kingdom the use of a carrying
chair was limited to specific ceremonial occasions, when ancient
and well-established practices would have been observed.

A carrying chair would have been the preferred method of
transport for the King, his family and other dignitaries, at least
until the New Kingdom. When the chariot was introduced the
Kings were quick to adopt the latest technological innovation as
their favoured means of transport.

(d) Donkeys

Whilst cattle were used as beasts of burden and are occasionally shown in tomb scenes performing this task, the main animal used in Ancient Egypt for this purpose was the donkey.

The African donkey lived wild in the desert from the earliest periods of Egyptian history and, even after domestication, wild herds still roamed the deserts throughout Pharaonic times.

It is apparent today that the donkey was first domesticated in the Late Predynastic and Archaic Periods (3150–2686 B.C.) and some of the earliest representations appear on slate palettes from this time. By the time of the Old Kingdom (2686 B.C.) donkeys are frequently shown in tomb reliefs, being herded in groups or being used as beasts of burden. The animals are easy to look after, they need little attention and can survive on little water and poor quality forage. Donkeys are also long-lived and can survive to their fortieth year or longer. They can also produce a new generation of beasts of burden, enabling new beasts to replace the old at little cost to the owners.

79. Donkeys from the tomb of Urirenptah. Fifth Dynasty relief from Sakkara

80. Old Kingdom scene of donkeys from Meir

Donkeys were used for threshing corn, by being made to walk over the harvested crop. They are shown carrying corn sheaves loaded onto their backs. Often they are shown with their owners, steadying the large loads, which must have been bulky, as well as heavy. On some occasions net panniers are suspended on either side of the donkey's back.

Many scenes on tomb walls show herds of donkeys with their foals. A certain status in society was no doubt achieved by the number of domesticated donkeys owned by one individual. The peasants are shouting at them, often in coarse terms, and their words are written in hieroglyphs above the scenes. If a donkey refused to work, it took three or four men and much encouragement with sticks to persuade it to continue. (Nothing has changed over the centuries in this respect, and donkeys who need such "encouragement" can still be seen in Egypt today).

It was the donkey which was used for all long distance, overland transport. Large caravans would tread the desert roads,

81. Donkey and driver, from a painting in the tomb of Panehsy at Thebes

96

going from water-point to water-point on the journey. The donkeys maintained the trade routes to other countries and carried the gold and minerals from the mines.

Today the donkey is still used for carrying crops over short distances and they are also ridden by their owners. The Ancient Egyptians did not appear to like riding donkeys, although we know that they were ridden by the Syrians. The Egyptians preferred to go on foot, or so the tomb reliefs would have us believe. These tomb scenes cover a multitude of domestic activities, but do not show every aspect. It is likely that the Egyptian artists may have found it difficult, within their artistic conventions, to show a man riding on the back of a donkey.

Riding on the back of a donkey is not always comfortable and certainly not very dignified (although if the donkeys were a rare and expensive commodity, this could have contributed some measure of status, if not dignity). The rider has to sit well back on the donkey with his weight directly above the hips of the animal. This also leaves sufficient room in front of the rider for small loads to be carried, as can still be seen today in Egypt.

Scenes survive from tombs which show people riding in a litter on the backs of one or two donkeys, which must certainly have been an uncomfortable and jolting experience. This, combined with the fact that donkeys can be amazingly stubborn, must have made for some eventful and memorable journeys. It is possible that the few representations of donkey-litters show old or infirm occupants of the litters. Transportation in such a litter may have been the only way for the tomb owner to oversee his agricultural activities. Such scenes do not appear in later periods, where other

82. Boy on a donkey
at Gurnah

methods of transport were available. The litters appear to be strapped to the donkey's back and the occupants either sit or kneel in them. The scenes show no signs of any padding or cushions, which must have been present in reality to make the ride slightly more comfortable.

The donkey is not held in very high regard in modern Egypt and this seems to have been the case in ancient times too. The donkey was sometimes thought of as the manifestation of the God Seth and was seen as being essentially evil. In fact, the unusual features of the God Seth, which are usually associated with some species of dog, bear more than a passing resemblance to some of the early representations of donkeys.

The hieroglyph for "donkey", shows the animal with a knife between the shoulders, presumably to remove any evil influence. The Egyptian word for donkey was *eeyore*.

The introduction of the horse to Egypt, during the New Kingdom, probably did little to reduce the importance of donkeys.

Scenes from the campaigns of Ramesses II against the Hittites show the army in camp. Donkeys are present in large numbers with loaded panniers, which were used to carry the supplies and equipment needed by the army. This would have included carrying food for the chariot horses.

The horse was used for specific and limited purposes and the donkeys remained the main beast of burden, which laboured all over the country in the fields and which, quite literally, carried the wealth of the nation on its back.

83. A nobleman on a donkey litter

It was not until the introduction of the camel that the importance of the donkey diminished. It is generally thought that camels were introduced into Egypt after the Dynastic Period, and, as such, they are not included in the methods of transport studied here. Absence of evidence cannot always, however, be construed as evidence of absence and a recent discovery at Qasr Ibrim in Nubia indicates that camels may have been on that site as early as 1000 B.C.. Future finds may help to clarify the position.

(e) Horses

The much-repeated theory is that the horse was introduced into Ancient Egypt by the so-called Hyksos or Shepherd Kings who invaded Egypt around 1600 B.C.. There is nothing really to support even the idea of an invasion as such and nothing to link the introduction of the horse to any invasion by foreigners.

We do know that horses and chariots were being introduced to the whole of the ancient Near East from the beginning of the seventeenth century B.C. and that towards the end of the period of the Hyksos rule, they appeared in Egypt, having been adopted following contact with Palestine around 1600 B.C.

The Egyptians adopted the Semitic names for both the horse and chariot, "susim" and "merkabot", but for the horse, a new Egyptian name was also used, which perhaps sums up the Egyptians' thoughts on encountering the horse for the first time: translated it means "the beautiful".

The horse arrived too late in Egyptian history to be included in the pantheon of Gods. One can but wonder what role the horse would have had, if it had been a native Egyptian animal. At the time of the New Kingdom, Egypt became influenced by the religions of other countries and horses were associated with the Canaanite Goddess, Astarte, who was called the "Mistress of Mares". Surviving painted scenes of a woman riding on a horse are thought to represent Astarte.

Horses were small by modern standards and Arab-like in appearance. Using the yoke measurements of the surviving chariots, an average height of about 1.35 metres (thirteen and a half hands) has been calculated.

The horse was introduced in conjunction with the chariot and it was this partnership which impacted greatly on the early New Kingdom and the expansion of the Egyptian Empire.

No training manuals survive for the horse owners, but it is assumed that the nobility would all have been trained from an early age in the use of the chariot for hunting and warfare and in the care and training of the valuable horses. Experienced charioteers would train others and we know that there was a Royal appointment of "Master of the Chariots".

Horses were clearly much loved and prized possessions. Amenhotep II, whilst still a prince, is said to have adored his horses and was "conversant with their training, having close acquaintance with their disposition." Ramesses III is recorded "inspecting the horses which his own hands have trained". The royal horses who pulled the King's chariot were given grandiose names. Those which pulled Ramesses II at the battle of Kadesh in 1275 B.C., were called "Victories in Thebes" and "May Mut be Satisfied".

84. A horse. After a painting from the tomb of Thanuny at Thebes

Surveys near the site of the palace of Amenhotep III at Malkata have revealed a straight stretch of desert from which all large stones and boulders have been removed. Four kilometres long and one hundred and twenty metres wide, this area may have been used as a training ground for the charioteers and horses. Unlike Ancient Rome, as far as we know, there were no formalised sporting competitions such as chariot races, but it is more than likely that horse breeders and owners would be keen to show that they possessed the fastest horses and could drive their chariots better than anyone else. This site at Malkata would have been ideal for such events.

85. Female figure riding a horse, possibly the Goddess Astarte

The horse adapted well to the climate of Egypt and herds were raised in the fertile Delta area. Stud farms flourished and the stock was often improved by gifts to Pharaoh of new horses from the Asiatic kings. Stable blocks were attached to most of the great palaces and estates and the horses were well cared for.

Burials of horses are rare, but Senenmut, an important courtier from the time of Queen Hatshepsut (1498–1483 B.C.) had his horse buried near his tomb. It must be presumed that this horse died a natural death, for there is no evidence or implication that the horse was killed to be included as part of the burial of Senenmut.

Senenmut's horse was about 1.5 metres in height (fifteen hands). The body was not mummified, but was simply wrapped in layers of linen, before being placed in a large, rough coffin. The horse was a mare and chestnut in colouring.

Apart from the figure presumed to be of the goddess Astarte, mentioned above, representations of the riding of horses are rare. Certainly we know that the Asiatic nobility thought it undignified to ride the horse and preferred to be pulled in a chariot, and this seems to be the idea adopted by the Egyptians. One New Kingdom model, however, now in the Metropolitan Museum, shows a rider, often identified as a "groom", on horseback.

No saddle is used and only a simple bridle. The representation of the colour of this horse, black with unusual white lines, has provoked some debate, as it is not clear if the artist has attempted

102

to reproduce the variegated pattern of the horse's hide, or if the white lines were chalked on to the skin of the horse as decoration. (The authenticity of this particular piece is being examined at the time of writing).

A scene from the Eighteenth Dynasty tomb of Horemheb at Sakkara shows a mounted rider, seated not on the horse's back, but directly above the animal's rear hips – the usual position for riding a donkey. Later representations show the riders in the more conventional position. This depiction may have been because the artist was familiar with riders on donkeys rather than riders on horses, and the scene may not portray the way horses were actually ridden. The horses are equipped with a bridle and reins, but have no saddles and stirrups. Cloths are sometimes shown on the horses' backs for the riders to sit upon.

Surviving scenes on the walls of the funerary temple of Ramesses III at Medinet Habu show mounted men. These are usually identified as messengers, but the fact that they are holding weapons (as does the mounted figure mentioned above from the tomb of Horemheb, who appears to hold a bow) indicates that horses may have been used in battle. It must be assumed that, at least in the early years of the Eighteenth Dynasty,

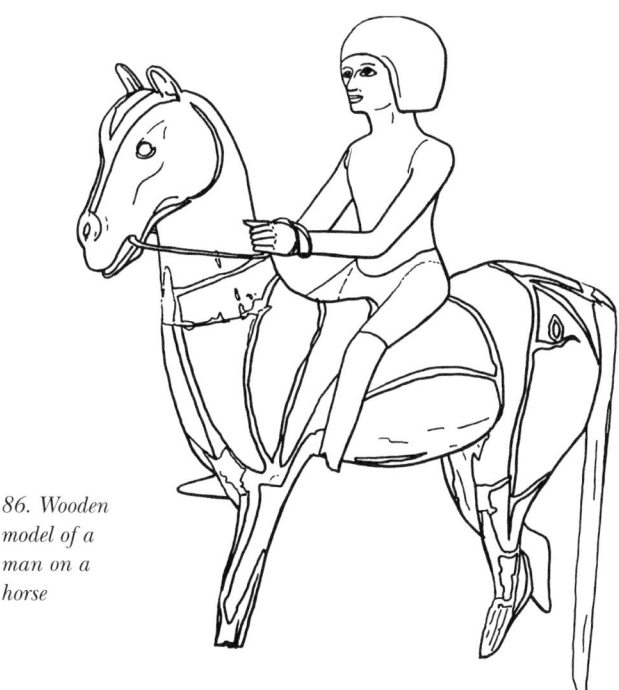

86. Wooden model of a man on a horse

87. Relief from the New Kingdom tomb of Horemheb at Sakkara, showing a man astride a horse on the so-called "donkey-seat"

the horse would have been considered too precious to risk in direct combat. Once, however, the "Egyptian" stock of horses had increased, the taking of risks with some animals would have been considered acceptable. It would have been surprising if some horses had not been ridden. If the Egyptians did not do so of their own initiative, once other nations led the way, the Egyptians would have had little alternative but to follow suit.

Certainly towards the end of the Dynastic Period, the riding of horses must have been common because of the influence of the Greeks and Romans, although there is no direct evidence of this from Egyptian sources.

(f) Chariots

Both the horse and the chariot arrived relatively late in Egyptian history. The Egyptians soon adapted the original Canaanite chariot design, to make lighter and faster vehicles.

It is possible that when first adopted by the Egyptians, the chariot was used for hunting and as a means of transport for the aristocracy when visiting their estates. Akhenaten mounted his "great chariot of electrum" when he marked out the boundaries of his new city for the god Aten at Akhetaten.

It was in battle, however, that the chariot really made its mark. The New Kingdom Pharaohs and their army commanders were quick to realise the full potential of this method of transport. Thutmose III (1504 - 1450 B.C.) the Pharaoh who pushed Egypt's boundaries further than any Pharaoh before or after him, rode in his chariot at the battle of Megiddo and was described as setting out "on a chariot of fine gold".

The use of chariots in battle is limited, as their use, and the use of the horse as a weapon, has never throughout history proved effective against well-entrenched, enemy infantry. Even Napoleon discovered this at the battle of Waterloo in 1815 A.D., when the British infantry, who had formed up in defensive squares, could not be broken.

The chariots were used as a swift-moving firing platform, from which arrows and javelins could be poured into the enemy. They were especially effective when attacking a disorganised enemy or one which was fleeing the field-of-battle. The use of chariots also greatly improved the means of communication during the confusion of battle and enabled the King to keep in touch with his commanders and the divisions of his army.

Many scenes showing chariots survive and are very detailed. The King is often shown in his chariot with his enemies trampled under the hooves of his horses. The conventions of the artists only show the chariots in profile, but from these representations alone we have a clear idea how they were made and used. Once again in Egypt, however, we are fortunate in having actual examples of the chariots, which have been found in the funeral equipment buried with their owners.

The vehicles are two-wheeled, light carriages, drawn by two horses.

By selecting woods most suitable to the task and, no doubt, learning much from the first chariots to arrive in Egypt, the chariot builders created vehicles whose main strength was their lightweight and flexible construction. Little detailed analysis of the woods used has been made, but they included elm, tamarisk and birch. The elm and birch are not native to Egypt and would have been imported.

The Ancient Egyptian woodworking skills are well known and evidenced by many superb examples of furniture. Perhaps this skill can best be seen in the construction of the chariot wheels, which are a triumph of woodworking and engineering. The wheels needed to be light, but also very strong and the ancient craftsmen achieved this difficult combination

The surviving examples of chariot wheels are all just under one metre (about three feet) in diameter. Slight details vary. The earlier examples from the Eighteenth Dynasty up to the reign of Thutmose IV, have only four spokes, whereas the later versions have six. Some reliefs do show eight-spoked wheels, although no actual examples of these have been found and the six-spoked wheel seems to have been the norm.

The spokes of the wheel are of a composite construction, each

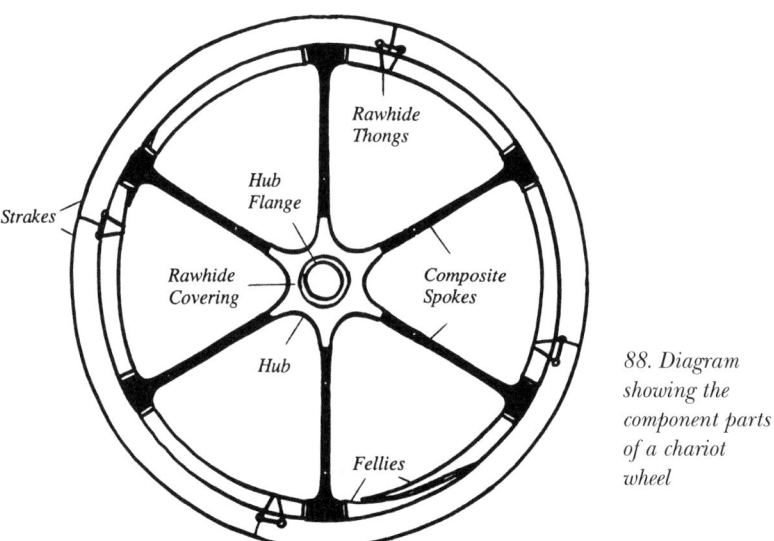

88. Diagram showing the component parts of a chariot wheel

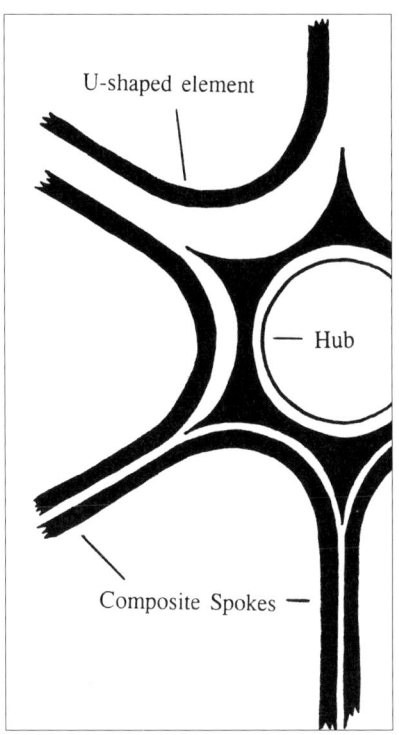

89. Diagram showing the construction of the spokes of a chariot wheel

spoke being made of two pieces of wood. U-shaped elements make up the wheel spokes; the two legs of adjacent elements, glued back to back, form one single spoke. The bottom of the U was either joined to the wheel-hub, or actually formed the hub. The spokes were slotted into the outer edge of the wheel and secured with rawhide. Most of the parts of the wheel were covered in rawhide too, which both protected the wheels from wear and also gave them additional strength.

The rim of the wheel was usually made from two pieces of wood (known as "fellies") of unequal length, scarf-jointed together and secured by "felly bands", over which were placed bent pieces of timber known as strakes. The wheelwrights stretched a green rawhide strip over the outer edge of the wheel. This served two purposes: firstly it provided a tyre, secondly, the rawhide shrank and tightened up all the elements of the wheel to consolidate the pieces. This is exactly the same way as modern cartwheels are made, except that the leather tyre is now replaced by a metal one. The leather tyres could easily be replaced when worn.

The width of the wheel on the axle was increased by adding a cone-shaped flange to the outer edge of the hub. This prevented

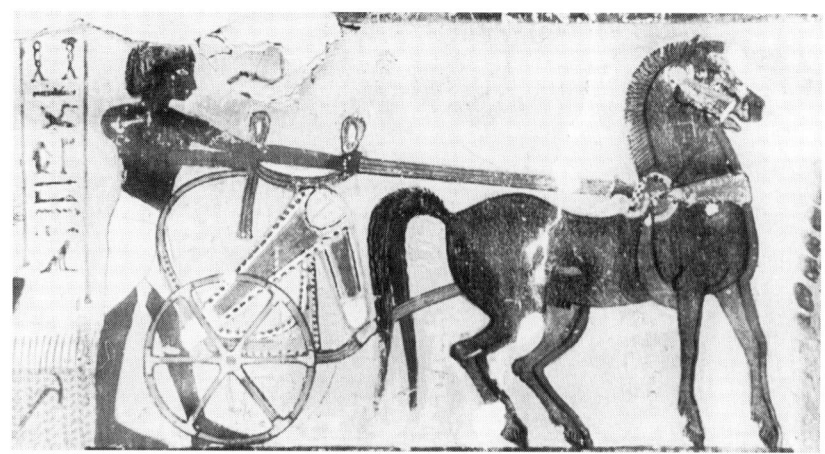

90. *Chariot and horses. Painting from the tomb of Nebamun*

91. *Chariot and horses. Painting from the tomb of Nebamun*

the wheel from wobbling on the axle. Grease kept the wheels freely turning and prevented undue wear on the joints, which in some cases were also sheathed in bronze. Linchpins inserted through the end of the axle kept the wheels in place.

The wood was bent by being dampened or by heating. Some woods, such as elm, can only be permanently bent by the use of heat or steam. Many scenes of chariot-making have survived, but this particular process is not shown. It is possible that some wood was specially grown for chariot-making; with branches being pruned and bent as they were growing. The use of naturally-grown timbers, but bent into the required shape by the hand of man, would result in a much stronger construction. Elm is a particularly strong wood. It is almost impossible to split because it has a twisted grain and it is able to withstand shocks. For this reason, elm has been used to make wooden wheels right up until modern times. The use of this imported wood shows that the Ancient Egyptians gained from the experience of wheel-makers outside Egypt.

The undercarriage of the chariot included a fixed axle to which the revolving wheels were attached, and the central pole.

The axles of the surviving chariots vary in length from 1.98 to 2.29 metres, whilst the wheels track at between 1.52 and 1.83 metres. This wide wheel-base meant that the chariots were remarkably stable, especially when turning.

The poles are 2.40 to 2.59 metres long and are made of a straight-grained, artificially bent piece of wood. The pole attaches to the chariot body in a socket beneath the rear floor bar and is also held in position by being lashed to the front floor bar.

The other end of the pole connects with the two-horse yoke also made from artificially bent wood. Over one metre in length, the yoke has an elegant curve which was designed to sit neatly over the necks of the horses.

On each side of the yoke, two leather straps ran along the pole and were fastened to it about two thirds of the way down. These straps kept the horses even and also helped to re-enforce the yoke and the joint.

The bodies of the chariots are small, being only about 1.07 metres wide and only 0.46 metres deep – just large enough to enable two adults to stand side by side. The majority of scenes of chariots in use show a single occupant only, usually the King. The reins are tied around the King's waist, which leaves his hands free to use his weapons, usually a bow and arrow. Whilst this potentially dangerous technique may have been possible when hunting over known or prepared ground, it is doubtful if the King would attempt to drive the chariot alone and fight and command the army all at the same time. Ramesses II is shown alone in his chariot in the many reliefs of his famous Battle of Kadesh, but the accompanying text always makes reference to his charioteer, who must have driven the chariot for him.

The floor plan of the chariot body is D-shaped. The rear of the body, the straight side of the "D", is formed of a solid bar of timber set directly over the axle. The sides and front of the body are made of bent wood. The floor was made from thongs of leather. The flexible construction of the floor was light and also acted as a form of shock absorber, when the chariot was driven over rough ground.

92. Tutankhamun in his chariot. Detail of a painted chest found in his tomb

The sides and front of the body are enclosed by rails of bent wood. The chariots intended for use in war had more solid sides made from either wood or laminated linen or leather, often given a plaster and gilt decoration. The hunting and sporting models had open sides. The chariot of Yuya has open sides, which could be filled by special leather hangings. The side and front rails also provided a ready hand-hold. It must have been essential under many driving conditions for the driver and other occupant of the chariot to have a secure hold. The back of the body was generally left open.

The wide wheel-base, the positioning of the weight of the chariot body and of its occupants directly above the axle, and the lightness and flexibility of construction made the chariots fast and extremely manoeuvrable.

Additional equipment found with the chariots and shown in scenes on the walls of temples and tombs included bow cases, quivers for arrows, javelin cases and also a pouch for supplies. This pouch may have contained items such as spare thonging for emergency repairs, or perhaps food and water for the charioteer.

All these pieces of equipment, many fitted with copper staples,

110

could be lashed to the chariot body. The tomb of Tutankhamun contained examples of bow cases, quivers and the bows and arrows used by the King.

Several actual examples of chariots have been found in tombs, which enables Egyptologists to compare the accuracy of the artistic representations of chariots with the chariots themselves. In paintings and reliefs, the chariots are always shown in profile and, whilst the proportions are accurate, one important thing which could not be deduced from these scenes, but which is apparent from the chariots themselves, is their width. Their track (width of the axles) is much wider than that of other ancient chariots. Also evident from the actual examples is that the body is normally open at the rear.

The complex harnessing used for the horses is clearly detailed in reliefs and paintings, and has been confirmed by the surviving examples (albeit fragmentary in most cases) found. It is thus possible to see how the horses were used with the chariot. (Titles of more detailed and technical books giving details of the harnessing, are included in the bibliography). The charioteer and his pair of horses would need to train together closely over a long period to be able to work effectively as a team and for the horses to recognise their driver's commands.

The horses themselves were equipped with brightly-coloured cloths to cover their backs and their bridles were adorned with ostrich feathers. In their brightly painted and gilded chariots and wearing their best clothes and jewellery, the chariot owners can have had no better way of proclaiming their wealth and status in society. The Egyptian chariot was the "Rolls Royce" of the ancient world, able to impress the native Egyptians and to instil fear in their enemies.

The Florence Chariot:

The first chariot to be found relatively intact was discovered at Thebes in 1829. The find was never properly recorded and at the time little was known about the conservation of ancient materials.

The wheels have only four spokes, as compared to all the other chariots which have survived, which have six spokes. It is presumed that this chariot pre-dates the other known examples

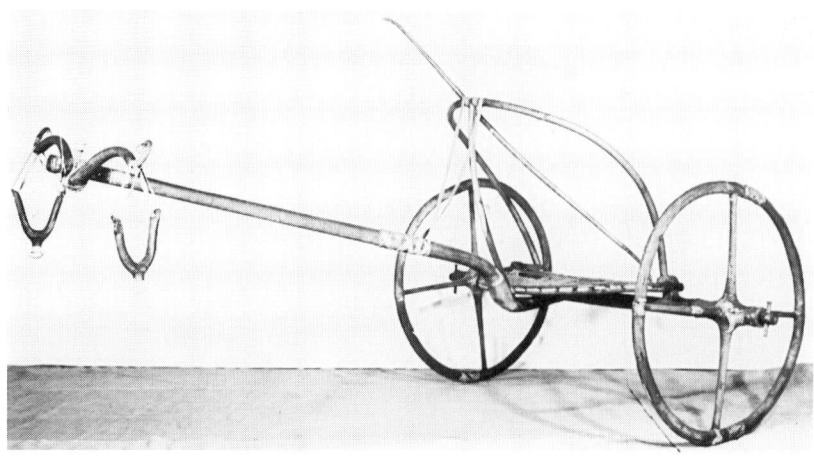

93. The Florence chariot

(probably dating to the early years of the Eighteenth Dynasty) and that a six-spoked construction was later found to be much stronger.

There would appear to be numerous recent patches in the fabric of the chariot, which indicates that the chariot was not well preserved when it was found and was substantially restored. It is also possible that the transportation and handling of the chariot caused damage to the fragile object. It is known that the leather tyres have not survived today, but any fragmentary remains of tyres might have been removed to present a "clean" object for display in the Museum. Consequently it is difficult to be certain that the appearance of the chariot today is the appearance which it would have had in antiquity.

The sides of the chariot are open; we now know that these are likely to have been fitted with leather panels – which in this case, have not survived.

With the discovery of other examples, various anomalies have come to light which may be as a result of restoration or may show an ancient evolution in the design. Nevertheless, the Florence chariot is still an important object.

The main dimensions are: body width 0.97 metres, axle length 1.99 metres, wheel diameter 1.0 metres, pole length 2.53 metres.

Chariot body found in the tomb of Thutmose IV:

When the tomb of Thutmose IV in the Valley of the Kings was discovered in 1903 by Theodore Davis and Howard Carter, only fragments of what had been splendid pieces of funerary equipment were found. One of the largest surviving objects from the tomb was the badly damaged body of a chariot. This chariot body only hinted at the splendour of the chariots which Carter was to discover nineteen years later in the tomb of Tutankhamun.

94 and 95.
Chariot body from
the tomb of
Thutmose IV

96. Detail of the decoration on the chariot body of Thutmose IV

Made of a wooden framework and panelling the body is 0.86 metres high, 0.52 metres deep (front to back) and 1.03 metres wide. All the surfaces are covered with fine linen and canvas covered in stucco plaster, into which elaborate scenes and ornamentation have been modelled in low relief.

The pictorial scenes are on four panels, two inside and two outside the body; they are divided by non-pictorial decorative panels. Howard Carter made detailed drawings of the scenes: the two exterior panels show the King mounted in his chariot and wielding a bow in one scene and an axe in another, confronting his enemies and causing havoc and destruction.

114

97 and 98. Drawing by Howard Carter
of the decoration of the exterior of the
left and right sides of the body of the
chariot of Thutmose IV

99. Drawing by Howard Carter of the decoration of the interior of the left side of the body of the chariot of Thutmose IV

The interior scenes, which are both almost identical, show the King as a sphinx, trampling over his northern and southern enemies. The hawk-headed god Montu stands behind the King. All the surfaces were originally covered in gold or possibly silver, but all the metal has been stripped away by robbers. The details of the decoration are, however, still clear from the plaster layer.

The survival of the coat of plaster and decoration of the chariot body prevents a detailed examination of the method of construction and materials used, but it appears to be very solid and this chariot may well have been designed for use in battle. This was a time when Egypt had a large, newly-founded empire and where the Kings were constantly fighting to protect their boundaries.

If the details of the scenes shown on the side of the chariot body are accurate, the wheels which were provided for the chariot body would have been made with eight spokes, which would have made them very strong, but still light, quite suitable for riding over unprepared ground. No trace of the wheels of this chariot were found in the tomb. Presumably they had been stolen, or had been removed in ancient times by the Necropolis priests when they cleared the tombs following previous robberies.

The tomb was robbed and resealed as early as the reign of King Horemheb, one hundred years after the burial of Thutmose IV. The complex and costly construction of the chariot wheels may have meant that they could have been re-used, but if they were covered in gold, as is most likely, they were probably destroyed to retrieve the precious metal.

The Chariot of Yuya:

Yuya was the father of Queen Tiye, Great Wife of Amenhotep III. A chariotry officer, he also held priestly titles in the temple of the god Min at Akhmim. With the marriage of his daughter to the King, Yuya and his wife Thuya were given favours by the King and Yuya was appointed Commander of the Chariots.

When Yuya and Thuya died around 1365 B.C., they were given the rare honour of a tomb in the Valley of the Kings. The tomb was discovered by Theodore Davis in 1905. Although it had been robbed in antiquity, the great proportion of the funerary equipment survived, including two magnificent sets of coffins enclosing the well-preserved mummies of Yuya and Thuya. It was fitting that a chariot was included in the funerary equipment of the Commander of Chariots. It was found at one end of the small burial chamber on top of a layer of pots. The pole of the chariot had been broken off, presumably by robbers, or possibly even at the time of burial, when those responsible for stacking all the objects in the small chamber may have found it easier to manoeuvre the chariot without its pole.

100. Chariot found in the tomb of Yuya and Thuya

In many respects, this chariot is similar to the examples found in the tomb of Tutankhamun, but it is at least fifty years earlier in date.

The body of the chariot is made of wood overlaid with canvas which has been plastered and gilded. The floor of the body is made from woven leather straps, over which was placed a piece of red leather which formed the floor of the chariot when found. This piece of leather was very brittle and little of it remains today.

The open spaces of the chariot body were originally filled in with pieces of red leather. Only one piece still remains in place at the rear of the chariot. All the other pieces were, according to James Quibell, who catalogued the finds in the Cairo Museum, ripped off in antiquity by the robbers and the few fragments which have survived proved too brittle to restore. Why robbers would want to rip off these pieces of leather when they were surrounded by objects of much greater value must remain a mystery, if Quibell was correct in his assumption. It is more likely that the leather quickly deteriorated in the tomb and disintegrated and that the pieces simply fell from the chariot. These red leather aprons were edged with a strip of green appliqué leather.

The inside of the chariot body is painted green and the outside is covered with gilt decoration, laid over a layer of plaster. The entire surface is decorated in relief, although the outlines appear indistinct, as if they were carved whilst the plaster was still moist. The main decorations are floral and geometric designs, but at the

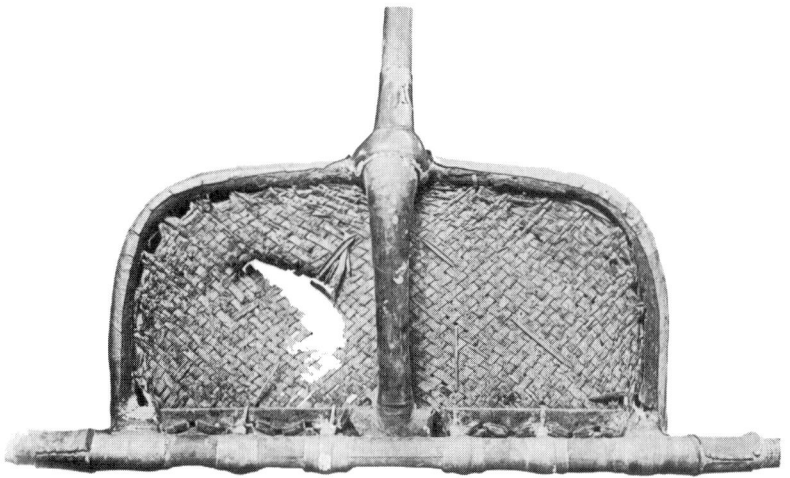

101. Detail of the floor of the body of the chariot found in the tomb of Yuya and Thuya

118

front of the body there is shown a large floral bouquet with an antelope on either side of it – perhaps some allusion to the hunting use of the chariot.

The rear of the chariot body is partly enclosed, unlike all the other surviving examples. It is not known if this was a common variation of design, as paintings and reliefs do not allow us a view of the rear of the chariot body and there are too few other surviving chariots to be able to draw any firm conclusions.

The six-spoked wheels have been fitted with red leather tyres, placed over two inner tyres made of coarser leather. The outer tyre shows little signs of any wear, but this type of tyre could be easily replaced and the chariot may have been fitted with new tyres for the funeral. The wheel rims are made from two pieces of wood, with one piece forming approximately five-sixths of the rim.

Solidified lubricant from the axle was found. Tests on the substance proved inconclusive, but it is presumed that the main ingredient was some form of animal fat. Sand found in the lubricant may indicate that the chariot was actually used.

The chariot is small in size and it could not be pulled by the usual full-sized horses. It is possible that this chariot may have been made specially for funerary use and could be considered a large-scale "tomb model". It is equally possible that smaller scale chariots were made and it is tempting to think that as Commander of the Chariots, Yuya would have been responsible for teaching the charioteer's skills to the princes of Amenhotep III, which would include Amenhotep IV (Akhenaten) and that

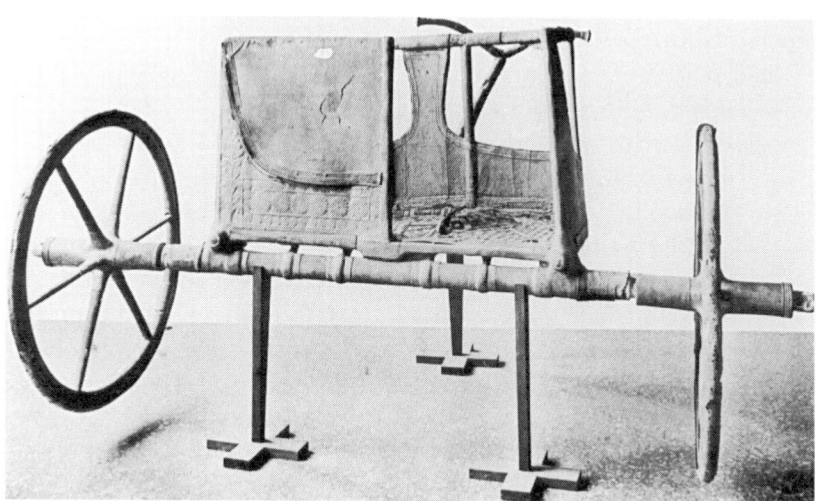

102. Rear view of the chariot found in the tomb of Yuya and Thuya

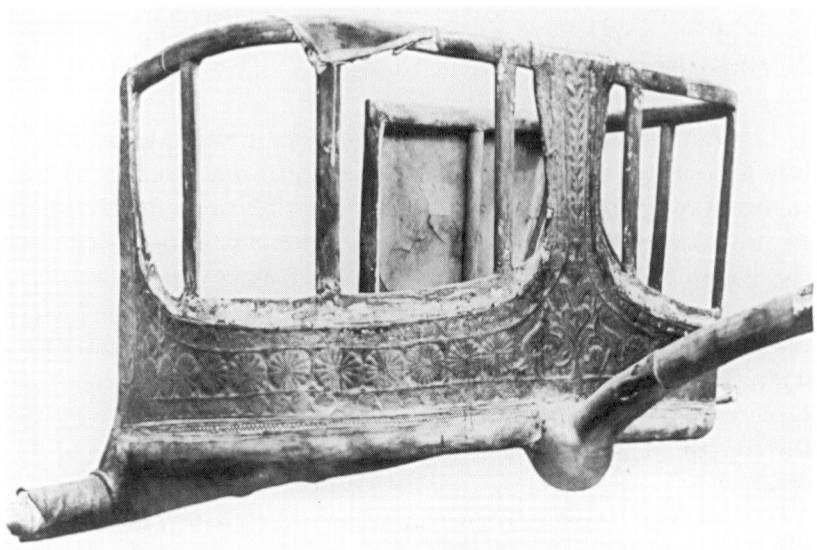

103. Detail of the body of the chariot found in the tomb of Yuya and Thuya

this reduced-scale chariot was used for this purpose. It could also have been used by the young Princess Sitamun, the eldest daughter (and later wife) of Amenhotep III. Chairs belonging to the Princess were found amongst the other funerary items from the tomb of Yuya and Thuya. This might explain the partly enclosed body, which would make the vehicle much safer for novice riders. When Yuya died, this chariot may no longer have been needed, or may have been nearing the end of its working life and was available for use in the afterlife, when its exact size may not have been considered important.

When new, the chariot would have presented a colourful appearance, with its gilt decoration and red and green leather. Even today, with the red now faded to a deep pink, the chariot, as displayed in the Cairo Museum, is a spectacular object, which is the centre-piece of a new display of the funeral equipment found in the tomb of Yuya and Thuya. It is evident from the apparent lack of wear that the chariot was in excellent condition when it was buried. Perhaps it was given a last refurbishment in readiness for the final journey. It was probably carried to its final resting place, judging from the complete absence of any wear marks on the leather tyres.

The main dimensions of this chariot are: axle 1.92 metres, track 1.47 metres, wheel diameter 0.74 metres, pole length 2.13 metres and body width 0.90 metres.

A Wheel Fragment Found in the Tomb of Amenhotep III:

This unprepossessing fragment of a chariot wheel was found by Howard Carter in 1915 amongst the shattered remains of the funerary equipment of Amenhotep III in the latter's tomb in the Western Valley of the Kings. After the death of Lord Carnarvon, the wheel fragment was presented to the Ashmolean Museum in Oxford. This fragment enables the complex construction of the wheel to be clearly seen. In the complete examples found, the details of construction are often obscured by layers of paint or gold decoration, but on this fragment, none of the obscuring layers have survived which has enabled the construction to be revealed and the materials used to be identified.

The skill of the Egyptian carpenters can clearly be seen, in what is a masterpiece of elaborate construction and jointing. Using basic tools of bronze, the skilled craftsmen constructed the wheel from many different pieces of wood, selected for specific qualities, to create an extremely strong, but light wheel. The spokes of the wheel are made from elm, the flanges of tamarisk. It appears from close examination of the grain of the wood used in the spokes that the U-shaped elements are here formed from branched pieces cut from the tree, rather than from artificially-bent pieces of straight timber.

Although the chariots themselves were light, when they were fully loaded with two adults and sundry pieces of equipment their wheels must have had to withstand considerable pressure and severe shocks when travelling over rough ground.

104. Fragment of a chariot wheel found in the tomb of Amenhotep III: Ashmolean Museum, Oxford

The Chariots of Tutankhamun:

All the other surviving complete examples of chariots come from the Tomb of Tutankhamun, in the Valley of the Kings, which was discovered by Howard Carter and Lord Carnarvon in 1922.

Although plundered by robbers on at least two occasions, the tomb still contained a vast amount of funerary equipment and objects which the young King had used during his lifetime. Tutankhamun remains the only Pharaoh to be found undisturbed within the magnificent set of coffins in which he was laid to rest around 1325 B.C.

Included in the jumbled heaps of furniture and funerary objects were six complete chariots. Four were found in the Antechamber of the tomb and the remaining two in the room known as the Treasury. Carter, when cataloguing the contents of the tomb, gave the chariots the reference numbers A1 to A6.

All the chariots had been dismantled in order to get them into the tomb. This "dismantling" included the sawing through of the axles and the removal of the wheels. The component parts of the chariots were all stacked together, but no attempt had been made to reassemble them in the tomb. The tomb of Tutankhamun is exceptionally small, when compared with other Royal tombs in the Valley of the Kings. In the larger tombs, there would have been sufficient space to accommodate complete chariots.

As with most of the objects in the tomb, the chariots were well preserved, although most of the leather had decayed, which has made it impossible to reconstruct the exact form of the harnesses which would have been included in the equipment. The horses were controlled by either bitted bridles or a noseband, placed low on the head of the horse to exert pressure on the sensitive part of the nose. Four long reins, two to each horse, were attached to the ends of the mouthpiece of the bit.

The tomb also contained many elements of related equipment, although the exact uses of some remain obscure. These items include whips, fly whisks, and blinkers for the horses, all heavily decorated with gold and inlay. Various purely decorative elements were also found, such as gilded figures of hawks, with solar discs on their heads. These may have been fitted to the poles of the chariots.

Little scientific work has been done to identify all the materials used in the construction of the chariots in this tomb and the fact that many of the surfaces are covered with plaster, gilt decoration

105. Tutankhamun's chariots as discovered in the Antechamber of his tomb

106. Detail of the dismantled chariots as discovered in the tomb of Tutankhamun

107. Dismantled chariots as found in the Treasury of the tomb of Tutankhamun

and paint would make identification of some of the elements difficult. Nevertheless, some woods have been tentatively identified, including elm, tamarisk and birch. None of these woods are native to Egypt and would have had to have been imported.

Two of the chariots (A1 and A2) were instantly recognised by Carter as "State Chariots" because of their splendid decoration. Gold and coloured inlay was lavishly used over a backing of plaster. These are the chariots Tutankhamun would have used for parade and ceremonial occasions when he mounted his "Chariot of Gold".

Both these state chariots were found dismantled in the southeast corner of the Antechamber of the tomb. They are made using a wooden framework with a thong mesh flooring. The sides have been filled in with thin wood which has been overlaid by a thick coating of canvas, gesso and gold. Both the outside and inside of chariot A1 is decorated with bands of geometric patterns inscribed in the gold and areas of coloured inlay. A central panel on the exterior gives the names and titles of the King. The interior of chariot A2 has scenes showing the King as a Sphinx trampling his enemies, similar to the scenes on the earlier chariot of Thutmose IV.

The bodies of these chariots were relatively well preserved and required minimal attention by Carter, which included cleaning and the reattachment of areas of loose or damaged decoration. Only traces of the flooring, which was of leather, remain.

Chariots A1, A2 and A3 have an unusual double curved rail at the front, the exact purpose of which is unknown, but which may

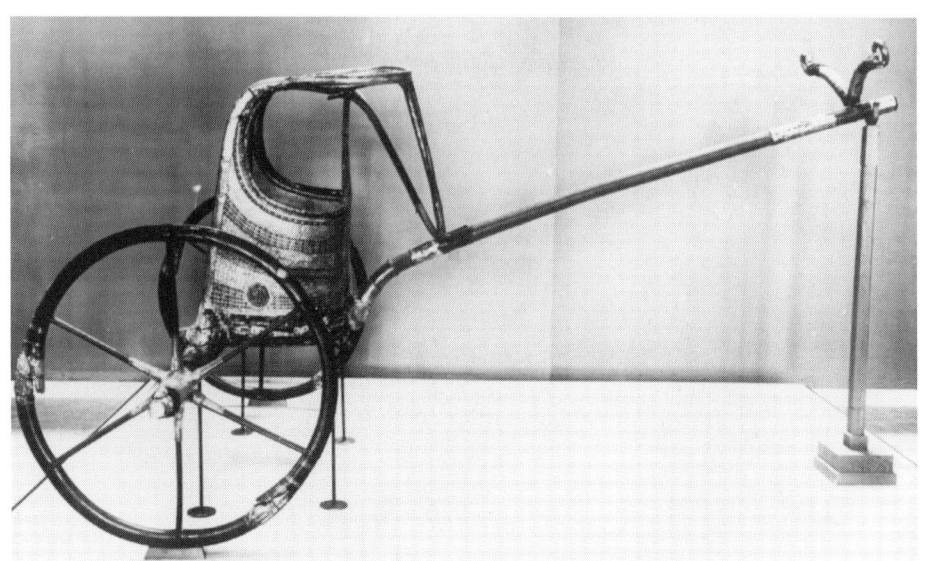

108 and 109. *Tutankhamun's state chariot (A1) as reassembled*

have been to help secure the various pieces of equipment needed, such as bow cases and quivers. A triple support runs from this double rail to the chariot pole.

Arthur Mace, working with Carter, noted that the floor of the chariot A2 was covered with a skin mat, possibly leopard skin, then two thicknesses of cloth and over this an imitation fleece of

110. Detail of the body of chariot (A2) from the tomb of Tutankhamun

111. Rear view of the reassembled chariot (A2) from the tomb of Tutankhamun

cloth, with tufts of linen sewn to both sides of the material, all of which would have helped to absorb any shocks when the chariot was driven over uneven ground.

The axles of both these chariots were still attached to the chariot bodies, but the left ends had been sawn through to allow them easier access to the tomb or to stack them in a more compact heap in a very crowded chamber.

Two other chariots (A3 and A4) were found in the jumble of the Antechamber. Both had also been dismantled. Chariot A3 was slightly less ornate than chariots A1 and A2, but was still covered in gold, and just falls into the category of "State chariot".

Chariot A4 is heavier in design and undecorated and may have been the practical travelling chariot or a war chariot. The wheels in particular are solidly built with thick strakes. The sides of this chariot remain open, which is unusual as there are no contemporary illustrations of open-sided chariots. As with the chariot of Yuya, the sides may have been in-filled with leather panels, which have not survived.

The remaining two examples (A5 and A6) were both found in the Treasury of the tomb. Once again they had been dismantled, but more so than the chariots from the Antechamber. The Treasury is a particularly small chamber, which was already full of boxes and the Canopic Chest, which meant that space for the chariots was limited and the dismantled parts were stacked in one corner. The fact that these two chariots were found in such a dismantled state meant that many of the construction details could clearly be seen. Both of the chariots from the Treasury are much lighter in construction than the other four examples from the tomb and they are gilded only in places. They were probably used for hunting. It is known that the King was a keen hunter, as there are many scenes on objects in the tomb which show the King hunting lions, gazelles and ostriches.

Only the framework of these two chariots survives. The floors are missing and any leather sides have been lost.

Chariot A6 was reconstructed and is on display in the Cairo Museum along with the chariots from the Antechamber. Chariot A5 remains dismantled and is not on display but rests in the Tutankhamun Magazine in the museum, where it is available for study purposes.

All six chariots from the tomb of Tutankhamun are much lighter than the example from the tomb of Thutmose IV. This may either show an evolution in their design or perhaps indicate

112. Tutankhamun's gold ostrich feather fan, showing the King hunting ostriches from his chariot

113. Wheels from one
of Tutankhamun's
chariots (A2)

that none of the Tutankhamun examples were intended as war chariots. Constructed from bent wood held together by glue and rawhide, they are all light and flexible, with no metal or rigid parts which could be jolted loose.

Some damage was caused by the robberies in the tomb and many of the fittings, which were probably heavily gilded and portable, were stolen. The humidity caused great damage to the leather, which effectively melted. From the surviving fragments it is possible to determine that the leather was probably coloured (as with the surviving examples from the tomb of Yuya and Thuya) and in many cases was covered with gold.

The dimensions of the six chariots vary slightly: all are full-sized and the range of measurements is as follows; axles 2.13–2.36 metres, track 1.57–1.80 metres, wheel diameters 0.91–0.93 metres, pole lengths 2.43–2.60 metres and body widths 0.92–1.02 metres. The size of the wheels in particular appears remarkably uniform, although exact measurements are difficult as most of the wheels have become distorted slightly from their original shape.

Although all the Tutankhamun examples are similar, no one part of any chariot can be interchanged with another. Clearly each chariot was a custom-made individual item, greatly prized by its owner.

All the chariots found in the tomb of Tutankhamun were real vehicles, which the King used in his lifetime and which he took with him in death. It must be supposed that all the other later royal tombs had their full complement of chariots buried with their owners, but apart from the examples mentioned here, no

114. Relief from the exterior northern wall of the Hypostyle Hall of the temple of Amun at Karnak, showing Seti I mounting his chariot

others have, as yet, been found. Numerous detailed reliefs do survive, however, showing the great warrior Pharaohs, Seti I and Ramesses II riding in their chariots and leading their armies into battle. These and later reliefs show six-spoked wheeled chariots, similar to those of Tutankhamun.

(g) Sledges

The use of sledges to move large objects, such as building blocks and statues, appears early in the history of Egypt. A few examples of such sledges have been found, but it is not possible to ascertain whether they were used to move the stone blocks as none have been found in the correct context. However, circumstantial evidence indicates that they must have been used for this purpose.

The surviving examples are made of sturdy wood, with two runners, the fronts of which are curved upwards. The sledges were pulled by human power, or by cattle, often along specially prepared surfaces to make the moving of large and heavy loads easier. These "roads" feature wooden sleepers, placed horizontally across the surface, at fairly close intervals and set into the mud used for the road surface. The sledges were then pulled over these sleepers and friction was reduced by pouring water in front of the sledge. The water liquified the mud and the slurry produced lubricated the passage of the sledge and its heavy load. Examples of these special roads survive at many of the major building sites and the method of lubrication is illustrated by reliefs showing large statues being pulled along on sledges.

Sledges are unlikely to have been a practical way of moving objects on loose sand or on rough or unprepared ground.

A Middle Kingdom sledge was found at Dahshur, in connection with the funerary boats found there. Well-made, it was used to transport the boats across the sand to their final resting place.

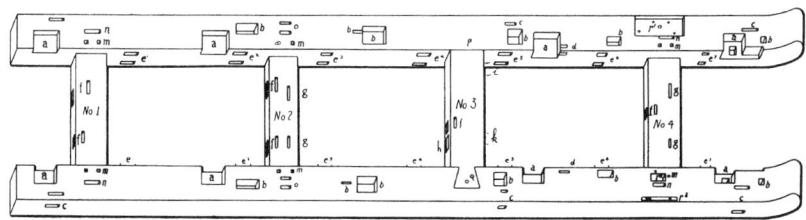

115. Wooden sledge from Dahshur

Six boats were found, so it must be presumed that this sledge made six journeys from the river or a canal to the tomb. Now in the Cairo Museum (CG 4928), the sledge is 4.21 metres in length and 0.80 metres wide. The wood has not been identified. Although a simple object, complicated woodworking techniques have been used in its construction, which include the use of dovetailed joints and mortise and tenon joints. All the joints are secured by wooden pegs. A number of different notches and holes have been cut in the sledge and these were used to secure additional cross pieces and upright posts to secure whatever object was being carried. Various holes were used to attach ropes. It is possible that this sledge had been in use for some time, to transport a variety of objects until it was used for the last time to carry the boats, after which it was then buried. Sledges had to be

116. The Dahshur sledge as displayed in the Cairo Museum

strong to withstand not just the weight of the object being carried, but also the considerable stresses of being pulled.

This sledge is on display in the Cairo Museum. Interestingly the third cross-piece appears to have fallen from its original place (probably some time ago). Replacing it in the correct position would have been difficult, as the sledge is mounted vertically, so the cross-piece has been fixed, incorrectly, at a lower level between the first and second cross-pieces. As it does not fit well in this position, with a dovetail slotted into a square socket, it has had to be crudely held in place with a length of wire.

Contemporary scenes of the transportation of large stones and statues are rare. One such scene, dating to the Twelfth Dynasty, shows a large alabaster statue of Djehutihotpe being pulled on a wooden sledge. The huge statue is securely roped to the sledge. The ropes are secured to bronze staples in the sledge and great care has been taken to ensure that the ropes do not damage the carved stone. Pads have been placed beneath the rope, where abrasion might have occurred.

The scene shows the sledge being pulled by one hundred and seventy two men, who are arranged in pairs along four thick ropes. It is not known if the artist represents here the exact number of men actually used, or if he simply filled with figures

117. Scene showing the transport of a colossal statue of Djehutihotpe, at El-Bersha Twelfth Dynasty

118. Transport of a building block. Eighteenth Dynasty, from the quarries at Tura

the space allocated for this scene on the wall. A man on the base of the statue pours water, or perhaps oil, from a pot to lubricate the passage of the sledge over the ground. Another man, perched on the knees of the statue, appears to be beating out a rhythm by clapping his hands to co-ordinate the efforts of the men pulling the statue, which could have weighed up to sixty tons. This statue of a nobleman is small in comparison to the many colossal statues of the kings which still survive today and which would have been transported this way.

A New Kingdom relief, from the rock quarries at Tura, shows a large block being transported on a sledge, but on this occasion it is pulled by oxen.

Examples of wooden rollers, which may have been used to move large stone blocks, possibly in conjunction with sledges, have been found at Sakkara and also at stone quarries at Lahun. Not many rollers are likely to have survived, as when they became too damaged to use they would have been used for firewood.

We know that the Assyrians in the eighth century B.C. used rollers to move large statues, but the use of sledges dragged across wooden sleepers would appear to have been the fastest and most used method in Egypt. Using rollers is a complicated procedure. Enough manpower would be needed to move rollers from the back of a moving block to the front. The rollers needed a great deal of attention to ensure that they did not jam or start to run sideways and would have been best used on a completely flat surface. Whilst adequate manpower was never a problem in Egypt, the easiest option would have been taken and the use of sledges seems to have been the preferred method of transportation of large loads over long distances.

What is interesting is that the sledge form appears on many surviving objects which would not necessarily have been expected to actually pull along the ground. Many of these objects are of a funerary or religious nature and include coffins and shrines containing images of the gods. The use of sledges for such items may have had some ancient significance, the origins of which are now obscure. In many cases the sledges on these objects are decorative and ritualistic, rather than practical.

The New Kingdom outer coffins of Yuya, Thuya, and Maiherpri all have sledges incorporated into their designs and funerary scenes on the walls of the burial chamber of Tutankhamun show the royal mummy lying on a bier and being pulled on a sledge by noblemen (although no example of such a bier was found as part of his funerary equipment).

It is unclear if the coffins on sledge runners were actually pulled along the ground. In some cases, it is apparent that the coffins were completed and assembled in the tombs and there is little, if any, evidence of the damage to the runners which would have been expected if they had actually been used. Those examples found in the Valley of the Kings would have needed to have been pulled a considerable distance, and the wear on the runners would have been extensive. In all probability these items would have been carried, if necessary by using wooden poles passed beneath them. The coffin of Thuya, whilst fitted with a sledge base, has two horizontal pieces of wood fixed across and beneath the runners, presumably to strengthen the box but making it impossible to use as a working sledge. Evidence from the tomb indicates that this coffin and that of her husband Yuya were taken to the tomb in pieces and assembled and painted *in situ.*

119. The wooden outer coffin of Yuya, showing the sledge runners (Fig 119)

120. Tutankhamun's Canopic Chest, showing the sledge base

The canopic shrine of Tutankhamun is also mounted on a sledge, which is heavily gilded. The surface is extremely fragile, and would have been so three thousand years ago. It does not appear to have been pulled over the ground, which would have damaged the decorated surfaces.

Many smaller objects from the tomb of Tutankhamun are also mounted on sledges. Again this must be for ritual reasons, as some of the objects are too small to pull along the ground without falling over. Clearly there is an "optimum" size for the use of a sledge, and it would appear to be practical for large, heavy or bulky items only.

One such small object, with a sledge incorporated as part of its design, is a gaming board. There may have been a practical reason why a sledge base was used for this as the board could easily be slid across a smooth floor, without disturbing the pieces. A board on legs, if moved, might have the tendency to "judder" across the floor and disrupt the game in progress.

Whatever the reason for the inclusion of a sledge in the design of numerous objects, the use of large sledges for the movement of large and heavy objects is certain to have been extensive through the whole of the Dynastic Period.

(h) Other Vehicles

Evidence for other vehicles in Ancient Egypt is scanty. Most of European history, and in fact the history of most of the world, has been greatly influenced by the use of the wheel, which is normally hailed as one of man's greatest inventions. And yet the wheel, whilst known to the Egyptians of the Old Kingdom, was not used extensively until relatively late, well after the civilisation had become established, and then only in a limited way.

It is likely that any form of wheeled transport would have proved to be of little practical use. Water transport moved people and goods to most parts of the country, donkeys reached the remote sites and the heavy blocks of stone were moved on the river in boats, and on land on sledges. It would have been difficult to build wheeled wagons strong enough to move these large blocks. (It can be argued that if the Egyptians had used the wheel, their buildings would have been constructed of much smaller blocks and probably, because of this, would have had a form differing greatly from what was actually built).

The most obvious form of transport rarely seen in Egypt for the main Dynastic Period, is a wheeled cart. Other, later

121. Gold model of a boat on a four-wheeled wagon from the tomb of Ahotep

122. Ox and a baggage
cart. From the battle of
Kadesh scenes of
Ramesses II

civilisations had better supplies of timber and animals (usually horses) to pull the carts. With little suitable timber, no horses initially, and no real need for wheeled carts, they do not feature significantly in the methods of transport in Egypt. The Egyptians must have encountered carts in their contacts with other countries and, whilst many foreign ideas were adopted, the cart does not appear to have been one of them.

Actual representations of carts in ancient Egypt are extremely rare. One unusual example which survives was found in the reburial of Queen Ahotep of the Seventeenth Dynasty, discovered in 1859. It is a model of a four-wheeled cart, which carries a boat. The model is all the more unusual and unique in that the boat is made of solid gold.

The wheels of the wagon are of bronze, fixed to a wooden body and are virtually identical in design to those familiar to us from the chariots. In this instance the wheels have four spokes which may indicate a date close to that of the Florence chariot which also has four-spoked wheels. The exact purpose of this model, and the nature of the boat it carries, is unclear and there are no comparable examples available. When first discovered, a second boat model made of silver was placed on the wagon next to the gold boat.

Similar wagons are shown in the tomb of Sobeknakht of the early Eighteenth Dynasty and also in a later scene (which dates to the third century B.C.) from the Tomb of Petosiris at Tuna el Gebel.

Scenes of the army of Ramesses II camped during his campaigns against the Hittites show oxen and wheeled carts. Looking not dissimilar to chariots, the carts have two wheels, but a slightly larger, square body. Pulled by oxen or possibly donkeys, these carts would have carried the supplies needed to support the men and animals on campaign.

By the end of the Dynastic Period, it is likely that some wheeled vehicles may have been seen in the Delta area, possibly in and around Alexandria, where Greek influence was strongest.

The Romans used wheeled vehicles extensively, but they had built up an extensive and well-built road network. Wheeled vehicles need a solid road, or they will quickly become bogged down in mud or sand. When the Romans finally invaded and captured Egypt, carts and wagons of various types will undoubtedly have been used to transport equipment for their campaign, but once in Egypt, it would appear that the invaders were quick to realise that the local methods of moving people and goods were efficient and practical. The river Nile remained the main highway through the country, backed up by an efficient road network.

Wheeled vehicles may have been used to travel and transport goods to the more remote sites, but whilst there was a good road network, the absence of paved roads may have prevented their extensive use.

EPILOGUE

From the actual surviving examples of the boats and chariots, it is easy to appreciate the tremendous skills of the boat builders and craftsmen.

The skills of these workers were not lost to man when the Egyptian Empire ended in 30 B.C.. For centuries before this, the Egyptians had invaded and traded with other countries and had been traded with and invaded by others. By trade and invasion, the Egyptian skills were passed to craftsmen in other countries.

By the time Rome finally captured Egypt and absorbed the country into its own Empire, the boat-building techniques and skills of the carpenters had already been seen, copied and adapted by the Romans, and before them by the Greeks.

In the intervening time between the ancient and modern worlds, much has changed, but the legacy of Ancient Egypt is still with us today. Many joints used by carpenters are exactly the same as the ones used in Ancient Egypt and some of the first examples of joints, some of which were very complicated, are found in the construction of the first large, wooden boats. The skills used by the boat builders, when they became familiar with the use of wood, were extended to the cabinet and furniture makers and these skills were essential to the master craftsmen who made the chariots.

The Egyptians developed their woodworking skills and techniques as far as their limited technology would allow, but it was a technology which was not to change significantly for nearly two thousand years until after the end of the Egyptian civilisation. Modern technology and materials have replaced many of the traditional crafts and revolutionised our methods of transportation, but in many parts of the world wooden boats are still made and wooden wheels are still used for carriages and wagons.

In Egypt itself, the place where many of the skills were first developed, the materials used for the construction of boats has changed and the motor car has replaced the chariot, but one aspect remains unchanged – the river Nile, which still remains the lifestream of the country.

The sands of Egypt no doubt have more secrets to reveal and many more examples of ancient technology remain, waiting to be discovered, either accidentally or as the result of organised excavations. These new discoveries will teach us much about the history of the civilisation of Ancient Egypt and also about the history of mankind.

Appendix: Glossary of Terms

Boats

Aft	The rear part of the vessel.
Backstays	Ropes to support the mast of a vessel, running from the top of the mast to deck level behind the mast.
Batten	A long, narrow piece of wood used to cover a seam or hold another piece in place.
Beam	The greatest width of a vessel.
Bevel	A flat surface which has been angled to make it fit with another piece.
Boom	A length of timber, slung by its centre in front of the mast, to support the foot of a sail.
Bow	The front of a vessel (also known as the stem).
Bulkhead	A vertical partition which separates one space or compartment within the hull from another.
Camber	The convexity of the deck beams.
Deck Beams	A cross member which supports the decks and also acts as a tie to connect the vessels sides.
Fore	Term referring to the front part of the vessel.
Frame	A cross-member extending across the vessel to support the planking or a curved timber which is attached directly to and supports the inside of the hull (also known as a rib).
Gunwale	The line of planks above the deck line on the side of a vessel.
Hold	The space below the deck which could be used for the storage of cargo.
Hull	The shell or body of the vessel.
Lifts	Rope supports tied to the ends of a yard or boom (and sometimes at other points along the yard or boom) and secured to the mast. Used to prevent the ends of the yard or boom from sagging.
Rowlock	A loop of rope attached to the gunwale to hold the oars in place whilst rowing.
Scarf	A tapered or wedge-shaped joint, used for joining two pieces of timber of the same thickness.

Sheer	The curve of the upper edge of the hull of the vessel.
Shell Construction	The method of construction when the shell/hull of the vessel is built before the frames and other internal strengthening members are fitted.
Stanchion	An upright post used to support another member. Usually short and wide as opposed to the dimensions of a pillar.
Stem Post	The papyriform timber which forms the highest part of the bow of a vessel.
Stern	The rear end of a vessel.
Stern Post	Corresponding to the Stem Post, the highest part of the stern.
Strake	A continuous line of planking from stem to stern.
Yard	A length of timber, slung by its centre in front of the mast, to support the top (and sometimes bottom edge) of the sail.

Chariots

Axle	A wooden pole which passes under the floor of the vehicle, to the ends of which are fitted the wheels.
Bent Timber	Timber which has been permanently bent, usually by artificial methods such as heating or wetting.
Body	The main part of the chariot which held the passengers. It includes the floor and walls of the body.
Felly	A segment of the rim of a wooden wheel, into which the spokes of the wheel are inserted. Egyptian chariot wheels normally have two fellies of unequal length, made of bent wood.
Ferrule	A ring or cap placed over the end of a handle or post, to prevent the wood from splitting.
Flanges	Conical tubes which were added to either side of the centre of the wheel hub and which help to stabilise the wheel on the axle.
Front Pillar	An upright piece of timber found at the front of the chariot body, which forms the main support for the framework of the front and sides of the chariot body.
Gearing	The undercarriage or running part of the vehicle, which includes the wheels, axle and pole.
Hub	The central part of the wheel, from which the spokes radiate.

144

Hub Band	A metal band which encircles the hub and which acts as both a protection against the splitting of the wood and as decoration.
Linchpin	A pin inserted through the end of the axle to keep the wheel in place.
Panel	A thin board or leather insert, which forms the outside covering of the framework of the chariot body.
Pole	The long piece of timber which is connected to the underside of the chariot body and which extends between the horses.
Pole Cap	The fitting for the end of the pole.
Rawhide	Untanned leather, used by the chariot makers before it had fully dried. On drying, the leather would shrink and would help to consolidate the joints and provide a tight and durable covering. Rawhide was also used to make tyres for the chariot wheels.
Rim	The outer framework of the wheel, made up of the fellies covered with wooden strakes and/or a rawhide tyre.
Strake	Bent pieces of timber, joined end to end, fixed over the Fellies and forming the outer edge of the wheel.
Sill	The main, bottom, rear timber of the chariot body, into which the rails were fastened and to which the axle was lashed.
Spoke	One of the radiating wooden bars which extends from the hub of the wheel to the rim. The spokes were formed of composite spokes in which the adjacent legs of two U-shaped elements formed a single spoke.
Trace	A strap which is attached to the end of the yoke and the base of the pole.
Yoke	A bar which runs across the end of the pole and to which the horses were attached. The yoke rested at the base of the horses' necks and was fastened to them by a strap.

Bibliography

BAINES, J.R. and MALEK, J. — *Atlas of Ancient Egypt.* Phaidon. 1980.

BLACKMAN, A.M. — *The Rock Tombs of Meir*, 6 vols. Egypt Exploration Society, 1914–1953.

BLUNDEN, Victor. — *The Solar Boat of the Egyptian Old Kingdom.* Private paper.

CARTER, Howard and NEWBERRY. Percy E. — *The Tomb of Thoutmosis IV.* Archibald Constable. 1904.

CARTER, Howard and MACE A.C. — *The Tomb of Tutankhamen,* 3 vols. Cassell and Co. 1923–1993.

CLARKE, Somers and ENGLEBACH, R. — *Ancient Egyptian Construction and Architecture.* Reprinted Dover Publications. 1990.

EDWARDS. I.E.S. — *The Pyramids of Egypt.* Penguin Books. 1947, Third ed. 1985.

EMERY, W.B. — *Archaic Egypt.* Penguin Books. 1961.

ERMAN, Adolf. — *Life in Ancient Egypt.* Reprinted Dover Publications. 1971.

FOX, Penelope. — *Tutankhamun's Treasure.* Oxford University Press. 1951.

GARDINER, Alan. — *Egyptian Grammar.* Third ed. Griffith Institute, Oxford. 1957.

GOYON, Georges — *Les Dossiers D'Archeologie.* Number 146-147. March 1990.

HABACHI, L. — *The Obelisks of Egypt.* Dent and Sons. 1978.

HANSEN, Kathy. — *The Chariot in Egypt's Age of Chivalry.* KMT vol 5, number 1. Spring 1994.

HARPUR, Yvonne. — *Decoration in Egyptian Tombs of the Old Kingdom.* KPI. 1987.

HEALY, Mark and McBRIDE, Angus. — *New Kingdom Egypt.* Osprey Publishing. 1992.

HEYERDAHL, Thor. — *The Ra Expeditions.* George Allen andUnwin. 1970.

HOFFMAN, Michael. — *Egypt Before the Pharaohs.* Routledge and Kegan Paul. 1980.

JANSSEN, Rosalind and Jac — *Egyptian Household Animals.* Shire Egyptology. 1989.

JENKINS, Nancy. — *The Boat beneath the Pyramid.* Thames and Hudson. 1980.

JONES, Dilwyn. *Boats. Egyptian Bookshelf:* British Museum. 1995.

JONES, Dilwyn. *Model Boats from the Tomb of Tutankhamun.* Griffith Institute, Oxford. 1990.

LANDSTRÖM, Björn. *Ships of the Pharaohs.* George Allen and Unwin. 1970.

LEHNER, M. *The Pyramid Tomb of Hetep-heres and the Satellite Pyramid of Khufu* Philipp von Zabern, 1985

LEPSIUS, Karl Richard. *Denkmaler aus Aegypten und Aethopien* 12 vols, Nicolaische Buchhandlung. 1849–59.

LIPKE, Paul. *The Royal Ship of Cheops.* BAR International, 1984.

LITTAUER, M.A. and CROWEL, J.H. *Chariots and related equipment from the tomb of Tutankhamun.* Griffith Institute. 1985.

LUCAS, A. *Ancient Egyptian Materials and Industries.* Third edition. Hutchinson. 1962

MASPERO, Gaston. *The Struggle of the Nations.* SPCK. 1896.

MURNANE, William J. *The Penguin Guide to Ancient Egypt.* Penguin Books, 1983.

NEWBERRY. P. *El Bersheh. Egypt Exploration Fund.* 1893.

PARTRIDGE, Robert B. *Faces of Pharaohs,* The Rubicon Press. 1994.

PATCH, Diana Craig and HALDANE Cheryl Ward. *The Pharaoh's Boat at the Carnegie.* The Carnegie Museum of Natural History, 1990.

PECK, William H. *Drawings from Ancient Egypt.* Thames and Hudson. 1978.

POSENER, Georges. *A Dictionary of Egyptian Civilisation.* Methuen and Co. 1959.

QUIBELL, J.E. *The Tomb of Yuaa and Thuiu.* Institut Français d'Archeologie Orientale. 1908.

REEVES, Nicholas. *The Complete Tutankhamun.* Thames and Hudson. 1990.

REEVES, Nicholas and TAYLOR, John H. *Howard Carter before Tutankhamun.* British Museum Press. 1992.

REISNER, George A. *Models of Ships and Boats.* Cairo Museum. 1913.

REISNER, George A. *History of the Giza Necropolis,* Volume II. Cambridge Mass. 1955.

SALEH, Mohammed and SOUROUZIAN, Hourig. *The Egyptian Museum Cairo.* Organisation of Egyptian Antiquities. Philipp von Zaben 1987.

SHAW, Ian. *Egyptian Warfare and Weapons.* Shire Egyptology. 1991.

STROUHAL, Eugen. *Life in Ancient Egypt.* Cambridge University Press. 1992.

TOOLEY, Angela M. *Egyptian Models and Scenes.* Shire Egyptology. 1995.

VINSON, Steve. *Egyptian Ships and Boats.* Shire Egyptology. 1994.

WESTERN A.C. 'A Wheel Hub from the Tomb of Amenophis III' *Journal of Egyptian Archaeology* Vol. 59, 1973.

WISE, Terence. *Ancient Armies of the Middle East.* Osprey. 1981. *KMT Magazine.* A Modern Journal of Ancient Egypt.

Index